CHICAGO POSTAL HISTORY

Selections That Honor the Collecting Interests of Richard McP. Cabeen

HARVEY M. KARLEN
—Editor—

Published by The Collectors Club
of Chicago, under the auspices of the
Clarence W. Hennan Memorial Publication Fund

1971

CONTENTS

PREFACE

Topics associated with Chicago postal history have engaged the attention of many philatelists through the years but most of these students are no longer writing or otherwise available for consultation. The reports of their investigations are scattered in bits and pieces in numerous periodicals and handbooks, most of which are out-of-print or inaccessible to those without access to a philatelic library. This book is an attempt to gather the many strands of postal activities of this single city and present the material in its historical setting. Through text and illustration it offers the current student of philately a survey of historical development and examples of postal usages during the first half-century of Chicago's growth.

This account owes much to the advice, help, and contributions of the Fellows of the Collectors Club of Chicago and to the others who made their materials available. The published articles and notes of Richard McP. Cabeen served as the core around which the material was organized. Permission to reprint these and other articles has graciously been provided by Harry L. Lindquist of Lindquist Publications, David Lidman, erstwhile editor of *Philately,* and the U.S. Philatelic Classics Society.

The Committee on Publications and Administration of the Clarence W. Hennan Memorial Publication Fund was responsible for establishing the guidelines of this study and for handling the many financial and other burdens of publication. My debt extends to the distinguished members of this body for inspiration and encouragement: Anthony C. Russo, chairman, Joseph L. Eisendrath, Charless Hahn, Paul C. Rohloff, Raymond Vogel, and Morrison Waud. Anthony C. Russo and Les Tirschell handled the photographic arrangements. Paul C. Rohloff is responsible for much of the layout work and for whatever artistic merit this volume contains. Joseph L. Eisendrath handled the many details necessary in the book's production.

The following names comprise an alphabetical list of contributors who generously loaned covers or supplied photographs: Sheldon J. Friedman, Leonard H. Hartmann, Mrs. Clarence W. Hennan, Alvin R. Kantor, Dr. Harvey M. Karlen, Douglas Lee, Mrs. Benjamin Newman, Charles F. Orgel, Floyd E. Risvold, Paul C. Rohloff, Melvin W. Schuh, Arthur Van Vlissingen, and Raymond Vogel.

My thanks are due to all of these persons who contributed to the development of the book, to the photographic editor of the Chicago Historical Society, as well as to Mollie B. Karlen who joined in this enterprise not only as my wife but also as proofreader and general assistant. Needless to say, responsibility for the substance of the book is mine.

Dr. Harvey M. Karlen
Cabeen House, 1029 N. Dearborn St.
Chicago, Illinois

December, 1970

RICHARD McPHERREN CABEEN, 1887–1969

Indefatigable writer, researcher, and collector, Richard McP. Cabeen has a prominent place in the first rank of American philatelic personalities. In his more than sixty years of philatelic activities he acquired memberships in local, national, and international societies and was the winner of highest awards for his writings and his other contributions.

Mr. Cabeen was born near Aledo in Mercer County, Illinois, attended schools in Seaton and Abingdon, and was graduated from the University of Illinois in 1909 with a B.S. degree in Architecture. He found employment with the architectural firm of Holabird & Roche (now Holabird, Root and Burgee) in July of that year and continued in this organization until his death in April, 1969. He took a leave of absence from November 1917 to February 1919, when he was chief of the engineering division of the Chicago district office of the Bureau of Aircraft Production. He assisted in the preparation of the Chicago Building Code, and he served on the architectural advisory committee of the Chicago Plan Commission for many years.

He married Blema Eulaila Meagher, of Canton, Ohio, on October 28, 1910. The Cabeens made their home at 1029 North Dearborn a fascinating display case for the many objects of art they collected together. In 1967, in joint action, they presented their home to The Collectors Club of Chicago, retaining the right to use the house during their lifetimes. Mrs. Cabeen died in July, 1969.

The first of a stream of Cabeen's philatelic writings was published in the October 1913 issue of *The Collectors' Journal.* Other articles led to a section in *Weekly Philatelic Gossip* in 1927, a weekly stamp column in the *Chicago Sunday Tribune* that appeared continually from September 11, 1932, until his death, a column for 18 months in *Popular Mechanics,* starting in 1937, the XIXth Century column in *Philately* in 1946–47, and numerous articles in *Stamps* and *Mekeel's.* He was also the author of articles in *The Stamp Specialist,* and co-authored with Dr. Carroll Chase the outstanding *One Hundred Years of Territorial Postmarks,* issued in book form in 1950. During the 1930's, Cabeen wrote a series of thirty booklets on various categories of U.S. stamps and of collecting, and this culminated in the publication in 1957 of his work, *The Standard Handbook of Stamp Collecting* by Crowell.

Cabeen's interest in Chicago postal history was a long one. He was a long-time friend and collaborator of Dr. Clarence Hennan, founder and president of the Collectors Club of Chicago for its first decade, and a pioneer student of Chicago markings, local posts, and whose collection formed the basis for the study in the 1941 Norona *Cyclopedia.* Cabeen's collecting interests included an outstanding lot of Chicago covers and these were often used to illustrate articles written by him or other authors. Several of Cabeen's Chicago writings are reproduced herein, and his other articles together with his voluminous notes form the foundation for much of the remaining presentations.

Arthur Salm
President, The Collectors Club of Chicago

CHICAGO: ITS POSTAL HISTORY*

Following the capture of Vincennes by George Rogers Clark, Virginia organized Illinois County but this lasted only until 1782, and the region thence had no form of government until after the organization of the "Northwest Territory" in 1787.

Marietta and Cincinnati were settled in what is now Ohio, and in 1790 Governor Arthur St. Clair organized the southwestern part of the territory as Knox county with its seat at Vincennes. This included much of Indiana and Michigan and all of Illinois and Wisconsin.

When Indiana became a territory in 1800, the western part of Knox county was

CHICAGO POST OFFICE in 1832, at the Forks of the river. Painting by Richard Richard. Courtesy The Northern Trust Co.

*Articles by Richard McP. Cabeen published serially in *Philately,* 19 August 1946 and 26 August 1946.

ILLINOIS.

ADAMS COUNTY.

OFFICES.		POSTMASTERS.	MILES FROM Wash'n	Vandal.
Clio		Amasa Shinn	959	178
Quincy	(c h)	Henry H. Snow	974	193
Rock Island		George Davenport		

ALEXANDER COUNTY.

America	(c h)	George Cloud	850	181

BOND COUNTY.

Greenville	(c h)	Lawson H. Robinson	801	20

CALHOUN COUNTY.

Belleview		Benjamin Mun	926	146
Gilead	(c h)	Levi Roberts	907	126
Hamburgh		John Shaw	916	136

CLARK COUNTY.

Bachelorsville		Laben Burr	696	86
Clark (C. H.)		Jacob Harlan	703	134

CLAY COUNTY.

Maysville	(c h)	John R. Taylor	740	46

CLINTON COUNTY.

Carlyle	(c h)	Charles Slade	802	30
De Witt		James M. Halstead	820	48

COLE COUNTY.

Cole (C. H.)		[No office 1st Oct.1830]		
Morton's Store		Charles S. Morton		
Paradise		George M Hanson	715	70

COOK COUNTY.

Chicago	(c h)	[No office 1st Oct.1830]		

21

Page from Official List of Post Offices of the United States—1831, *prepared by U.S. Postmaster General reporting no post office for Chicago in 1830.*

renamed St. Clair county but was limited to the southern part of the present state of Illinois. In 1801 this county was enlarged and included the site of Chicago. Illinois became a territory in 1809 and after various county arrangements, Cook county was established on January 15, 1831, with its seat at the "Town of Chicago," then only a name on a plat by James Thompson, surveyor, dated August 4, 1830. Cook county at that time included all of present DuPage and Lake counties and parts of Will, Kane and McHenry counties.

The settlement at the mouth of the Chicago river amounted to little until after the Black Hawk War and the removal of nearby Indians. Fort Dearborn had been built there in the early winter of 1803–04 and was garrisoned until the massacre on August 15, 1812.

From that date until July, 1816, when soldiers returned to rebuild the fort, only three

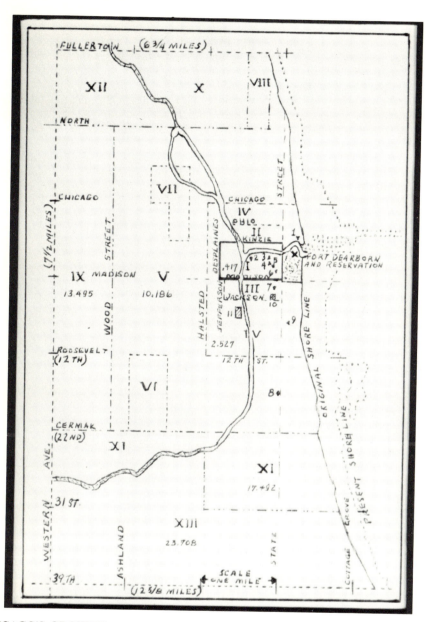

CHICAGO'S GROWTH 1830–1863. Area I is the original size of the village in August, 1831, with additions indicated by Roman numerals. The smaller numbers indicate locations of the city's post offices. Figures with decimals represent area of addition.

3

families resided on the site of the city. Until the troops came to garrison the new fort the victims of the Fort Dearborn massacre rested where they fell on the sandy dunes near Lake Michigan at 18th Street.

Fort Dearborn was not continuously garrisoned and was empty at the time of the Winnebago uprising in 1827, but was occupied by troops at the outbreak of the Black Hawk War in 1832. The last garrison moved out on December 29, 1835, and the last remnant of the post was demolished in 1857.

Politically the settlement was recognized in 1821 by the appointment of John Kinzie as a Justice of the Peace by the commissioners of Pike county. In 1823 his appointment was renewed but as of Fulton county. Later in 1823 the region became the 1st precinct of a newly organized Peoria county.

It may be assumed that the settlement had a population of at least 150 in 1831, for it was incorporated in the summer of that year under an act permitting communities of 150 people to set up local governments with limits not to exceed one square mile. The Board of Trustees first met and set up the government on August 12, 1831. This town of

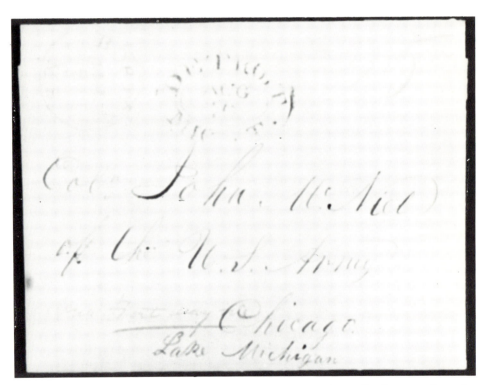

Boston origin folded letter dated JULY 25 (1822), bears red ms. "25" rate and routing "Via Fort Wayne." Letter carried to Detroit where forwarding mark was applied and then to Ft. Wayne by post office; on final leg to Chicago carried by regular army courier who shuttled between Fort Dearborn and Fort Wayne. Addressed to Col. John McNiel (sic).

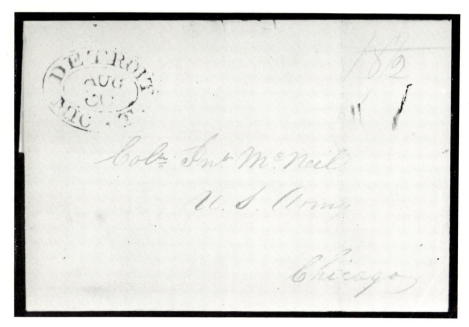

Detroit origin folded letter dated AUG 30 (1822), with ms. "18-1/2" rate. Addressed to Col. J. McNeil, U.S. Army, Fort Dearborn, Chicago. The second Fort Dearborn was built in 1816.

Chicago embraced three-eights of a square mile between State and Desplaines Streets from Kinzie to Madison Streets (area I on map).

On November 6, 1831, the limits were extended north to Ohio Street and south to Jackson Street so that the area was almost a square mile (see II and III on map).

On February 11, 1835, the Town of Chicago was incorporated and extended to include the tracts IV on the map. It now had an area of about 2-1/2 square miles. On March 3, 1837, it was incorporated as a city and included tract V and had a total area of a little more than 10 square miles.

Tracts VI and VII were withdrawn in 1843 but were re-annexed along with new tracts VIII and IX in 1851. The next expansion came in 1853 with the addition of X and XI giving a total area of 17-1/2 square miles. In 1863 during the Civil War the city plot was squared up by the addition of XII and XIII to give it a total of 23.7 square miles. Since that time various additions have been made until in 1940 its area amounted to almost 213 square miles.

The population in 1829 has been estimated at 60 persons. In 1831, it was 150 and in 1832, 600. The census of 1840 shows 4,470 inhabitants and that of 1850, 28,269. By 1860 there were over 100,000 and by 1870, over 300,000.

The first mail route to cross the Allegheny mountains was established in 1788 and reached west to Pittsburgh. Within a few years it had been extended to Louisville (1794), Vincennes (1800) and Cape Girardeau (1810). During this period there was communication, of course, with each army post and each fort may be said to have

5

established a postoffice with the commandant as postmaster.

Northern Illinois was still in the hands of the Indians and was not generally open to white settlement. Not until early in 1820 was there any postal service to the few settlers and traders clustered around Fort Dearborn. In 1820 the Postoffice department arranged for a monthly service between Fort Wayne, Indiana, and Fort Dearborn, and occasionally a sailing vessel from the eastern lakes brought mail from Detroit and other points.

The stories of the early postmen who carried the mail across Indiana or Michigan from Detroit or who traveled between Fort Dearborn and Green Bay are filled with the hardships of pioneer life. Each of these trips required as much as two weeks on foot, for at the start, the forests were so dense that it was difficult to guide a horse through the wilderness. At rare intervals mail arrived at Fort Dearborn from the south, coming up from Fort Clark at Peoria.

Messengers were not equipped with pouches at this time but carried a flat metal box covered with untanned deerskin. Alexis Clermont, the carrier between Chicago and Green Bay in the early 30's, has stated that the load averaged about 60 pounds and that his pay amounted to about $60 to $70 and that a round trip required a full month.

A little before this time, in 1826, David McKee used an Indian pony to carry the mail between Fort Wayne and Fort Dearborn. He proceeded on foot leading the pony, and his route was from Fort Wayne to Elkhart, then to Niles, Michigan and on to Fort Dearborn. This trip took 14 days but on special occasions could be covered in ten days.

The first postoffice in Chicago was established on March 31, 1831, with Jonathan N. Bailey as postmaster. The office was located in the old Kinzie house across the Chicago river from Fort Dearborn about where the east line of the present Michigan Avenue crosses North Water Street (No. 1 on the map). The site of this house is marked by a memorial plate on the balustrade.

This small log building was used as a residence until 1821 and then as a store by Anson H. Taylor in 1829 before it became the postoffice. It is perhaps worthy to note that this original postoffice was not within the incorporated village.

In 1832, John Stephen Coates Hogan arrived in Chicago and opened a store in a log building located about at the corner of the present Franklin Street and Wacker Drive. Mr. Hogan soon married the postmaster's daughter and the postoffice was moved to Hogan's store (No. 2 on map). For a short time Mr. Hogan assisted Jonathan Bailey in the duties of the office and on the departure of the latter with his family to St. Louis was appointed as postmaster, November 2, 1832.

Mr. Hogan led an active life for in addition to conducting the store and serving as postmaster he was a Justice of the Peace, alderman, deputy sutler at the fort, land agent, lieutenant in the Black Hawk War and a poet. He invested too heavily in real estate and was made bankrupt by the panic of 1837.

In 1831 there were two lines of stages between Detroit and Tecumseh, Mich., the Pioneer and the Opposition. From Tecumseh the mails came westward tri-weekly in summer by wagons to Niles, and thence to Chicago on horseback. In the winter mounted riders were used from Tecumseh to Chicago. By 1832 the traffic required daily stages to Niles.

At this time four post routes were in operation in and around Chicago: Route No. 46—Fort Wayne by Good Hope, Elkhart Plain, Goshen, Pulaski, Edwardsburgh to Niles, Michigan Territory, once a week, and from Niles to Chicago, twice a week, on horseback. The distance was 90 miles and the contractor was John G. Hall with pay at $175. Route No. 74 was to Vincennes by Palestine, Hutsonville, York, Clark C. H., Livingston, Paris, Ona, Bloomfield, Carolus, Georgetown to Danville, 120 miles, once a week from May 1 to November 1, in a two-horse stage, and the residue of the year on horseback. Also mails went from Danville to Chicago, 130 miles, once every two weeks. The contractors were Oliver Breeze & Co., and the pay was $600. Route No. 83 extended from Decatur by Randolph's Grove, Bloomington, Ottawa, Chestnut, Vermillion and DuPage to Chicago, 185 miles, once a week. The contractor was Luther Stevens and the pay was $700. Route No. 84, ran from Chicago by Romeo, Iroquois and Driftwood to Danville, 125 miles once a week. Robert Oliver was the contractor with pay at $600.

Red circle postmark dated JUL 16 (1835), with ms. rate marking. Letter written by J. B. Beaubien, Chicago pioneer, asserting his claim to the ownership of the site of Fort Dearborn.

The receipts of the Chicago postoffice amounted to $47 in 1832 and in spite of improved service it required 14 days for a letter to come from New York or Washington and five days or a little more for a letter from Detroit. Mr. Hogan was criticized for the lack of order in his office where the letters were left to lie on an exposed table until called for or until they disappeared. When his attention was called to the pigeon hole method of caring for mail, he solved his problem by nailing discarded boots to the wall by the soles with the bootleg serving as the mail container.

In 1833, Mr. Hogan had as an assistant or deputy postmaster, John Bates, Jr., who had arrived in Chicago the previous year. He took full charge of the postoffice and partitioned it off from the remainder of the building, then occupied by the business known as Brewster, Hogan & Co. By 1834 or 1835 the mail from the east had increased, so that it was necessary to substitute a wagon for the pony. This was operated by John S. Trowbridge under contract.

The road to Green Bay was surveyed in 1833 and trees blazed in the forests and stakes driven along the prairie trails. By 1834 it had been improved to Milwaukee with bridges over unfordable streams and with all trees cut down on the road for a width of two rods.

Roads to the west and south offered less difficulty for they crossed the open prairie, but in wet weather they became impassable ditches of mud. John T. Temple came to Chicago in July, 1833, with a contract to carry the mail to Fort Howard, or as it was popularly known—Green Bay. He soon secured a contract to carry the mail to Ottawa and made the first trip on January 1, 1834, in an elegant post coach bearing several notables. This route was the first leg of a recently authorized post road from Chicago to St. Louis.

In 1834 John L. Wilson was appointed second assistant postmaster, and later this position went to Thomas Watkins. Perhaps in another age they would have been clerks, but in the Chicago of 1834 with about 1,800 inhabitants, the office had first and second assistant postmasters.

The first advertised letter list appeared in the *Chicago Democrat,* January 7, 1834. It listed but one letter.

On January 11, 1834, the citizens petitioned Congress for completion of the post road to Detroit. The coach road came as far as Niles but the remainder of the journey was a nightmare. In the summer of 1834 the road was extended to St. Joseph, Michigan Territory, and a regular line of steamboats connected that port with Chicago.

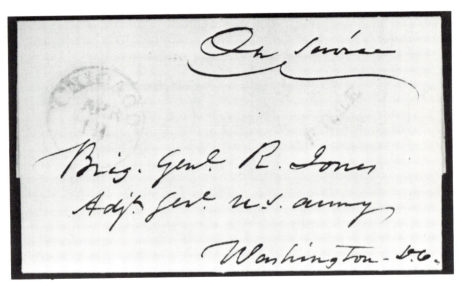

FORT DEARBORN "On Service" letter dated APRIL 17, 1837, with FREE. Letter written by Maj. Plympton regarding petition drawn up to deal with termination of streets at the Military Reservation.

By August 1834, four horse post coaches ran twice a week between Chicago and St. Louis, through Ottawa, Peoria and Springfield.

In September, 1835, Postmaster Hogan, announcing a new schedule of arrivals of mail, stated that postage for letters must be paid when the letters were taken out. There was to be no more credit and letters would not be delivered to others than those addressed without written orders.

On March 3, 1837, Sidney Abell was appointed postmaster. On June 3 he moved the office to the Bigelow building on Clark Street between Lake and South Water Streets (No. 3 on map).

In 1837, Frink and Walker took over the stage line to Ottawa and extended it. One stage reached Rockford, January 1, 1838, after a 24 hour ride.

In 1840 John Frink succeeded Dr. Temple as mail contractor. His stages, under the names of Frink and Walker, and Frink and Bingham, were well-known throughout the far west. The stage office was located at 123 Lake Street (old style) now about 81 West Lake Street, and later was moved to the corner of Lake and Dearborn Streets.

On July 10, 1841, William Stuart, editor of the Chicago American, was appointed postmaster, and on August 1, severed his connections with the newspaper. At once he moved the postoffice to a new site on the west side of Clark Street adjoining the Sherman Hotel (No. 4 on map), the north portion of the Sherman Hotel site. Through error this postmaster's name is given in Washington postal records as William Stewart.

In 1842 the Michigan Central railroad reached Ypsilanti, and five years later trains ran into Kalamazoo. Soon the rails reached Lake Michigan at New Buffalo. By 1852 this railroad had continued its lines into Chicago.

On April 3, 1843, Wells & Co., started a tri-weekly express to the east and two years later changed to a daily service. An advertisement in the *Chicago Daily Journal,* August 7, 1844, lists the cities on their routes and the rates of postage for letters, etc. For Wisconsin, Michigan and Ohio cities, the rates were 6-1/4 cents per letter, or one stamp per letter, with stamps at twenty for one dollar. New York state offices cost 12-1/2 cents, or two stamps per letter, and New England towns and a few others such as Newark, and Philadelphia, 18-3/4 cents or three stamps for each letter. Their local office was at the store of S. F. Gale & Co., stationers, 106 Lake Street, now about 60 West Lake Street.

In 1846, A. H. and C. Burley, who had been clerks for Gale, succeeded to the stationery business and also became the agents for Wells & Co. This concern was then owned by Messrs. Wells, Fargo and Dunning, but in 1847 passed into the hands of William C. Fargo and William A. Livingston and was operated as Livingston & Fargo. In 1850 it consolidated with other interests of Wells & Co., and Butterfield, Wasson & Co., under the title of the American Express Co. Its service was so superior to that of the post office that the newspapers often publicly thanked the company for its speedy delivery of news.

A mass meeting of Chicago citizens on January 6, 1845, sent a resolution to Congress demanding a reduction in the rates of postage and the abolition of the franking privilege.

The Chicago postoffice became a Presidential office in 1845 and Hart L. Stewart was nominated for the position of postmaster by President Tyler, but his nomination was not confirmed until February 3, 1846.

In 1847, the *Democrat* announced that the cheaper postage system had proved a great boon but complained of the lack of speed in the service. The same newspaper desiring to present the President's message as early as possible brought it 130 miles from Mattville, Michigan, in nine hours, with the result that it was received 36 hours ahead of the first copy to come by regular mail.

Although numerous projected railroads had a terminus in Chicago, this city never saw a locomotive until October 10, 1848, when the "Pioneer," a second hand engine brought in by the Galena Railroad arrived by boat, for service on its five miles of completed roadway. In this year also the first line of telegraph was completed into Chicago.

On April 23, 1849, President Zachary Taylor nominated Richard L. Wilson, publisher of the Chicago Daily Journal, as postmaster. With the next change in party administration, President Fillmore appointed George W. Dole, as postmaster, on September 25, 1850. During his term the postoffice was moved to the east side of Clark Street at Nos. 49-51, now 169-167 North Clark St. (No. 5 on map). At this time there were 29 postoffices in each county.

Increased business in the Chicago postoffice resulted from the cheap rates of 1851, but very little use was made of postage stamps at that time.

On February 9, 1852, the Michigan Southern railroad reached Michigan City, Indiana, and on February 18, the trains reached Ainsworth's (now South Chicago), 12-1/2 miles from the city. A fast team brought the mail on in 40 minutes. Two days later, February 20, the first train of the Michigan Southern and Northern Indiana R.R. (now Lake Shore & Michigan Southern R.R.) reached the heart of the city. At this period the section of the road between Buffalo and Toledo had not been built and the passengers and mail, etc., were carried the length of Lake Erie by boat. On May 21, 1852, the Michigan Central brought a train into the city by running from Grand Crossing over the Illinois Central tracks. Now it required only 41-1/2 hours for New York mail to reach Chicago.

On March 22, 1853, Isaac Cook became postmaster, with Charles S. Dole as assistant postmaster. In the following year H. A. Wynkoop succeeded Mr. Dole. On February 23, 1854, Cook moved the postoffice to 84-92 Dearborn Street, using the ground floor of a brick building of Randolph Street, now about 122-112 N. Dearborn St. (No. 6 on map). Meanwhile, the government had purchased a site for a Federal building at the corner of Monroe and Dearborn streets, and had started construction on a modern building.

What is thought to be the first local post in Chicago was established by William McMillan in February, 1855. The charge for a letter was one cent if prepaid and double if sent collect. Other local posts started up and lasted a year or so until all were abolished by Act of Congress.

William Price became postmaster on March 18, 1857, and held the office until Isaac Cook was reappointed by President Buchanan on March 9, 1858.

In August, 1857, the first steps were taken for the establishment of branch postoffices, but there were no results until five years later. By the end of 1857 the new postoffice building which was to occupy 82 feet on Monroe Street, and 163 feet on Dearborn Street (No. 7 on map) began to show above the ground. It cost $434,894, was occupied in November, 1860, and served for all federal purposes until destroyed in the great fire of 1871.

Sometime during Cook's term as postmaster a form of supplementary mail was introduced at the Chicago postoffice . . . The service was generally limited to eastbound trains leaving the city shortly after the close of the business day. Westbound trains of the time had only short runs and left Chicago much later in the evening with ample time for all mail collected in the late afternoon to be put aboard. Appropriate hand-

Post Office, Chicago, Ill.

May 14 1851

P. M. *New Haven Ill*

Sir : Your order for Blanks, of .... has been forwarded to **JEWETT, THOMAS & CO.,** *Buffalo, N. Y.,* who are the Contractors for supplying the same, and you will receive direct from them, by mail.

On reception you can compare the Blanks received, with this circular, and ascertain if the order has been correctly filled.

This Office is not authorised to supply other Offices with Envelope Paper or Stationery. You can procure for yourself what is necessary for the business of your Office, after using the Wrappers and Twine which come to your Office upon Letters and Packages, and charge it to the Department in your Quarterly Account.

Your order will be filled as follows :

Sheets, Mails Received,

    "   "   Sent.

    "   Account of Newspapers and Pamphlets received.

5 "   Accounts Current.

    "   Post Bills.

    "   Bills of Postage, or Affidavits of Official Letters.

Signature Post Bills are supplied to Offices which collect, in postages, Three Hundred Dollars or more, per annum.

GEO. W. DOLE P. M.

stamps were used to postmark this mail and they are always in demand by United States specialists.

John L. Scripps, of the Chicago Tribune, became postmaster April 1, 1861, having been appointed by President Lincoln on March 28. Mr. Cook refused to surrender the office until the end of the quarter.

On August 13, of that year new designs of stamped envelopes were received in Chicago. These were to replace the previous issue since so many were left on hand in southern rebel postoffices. New postage stamps, the issue of 1861, prepared to prevent rebel supplies from reaching the north, arrived in Chicago on August 20 and a notice of the 21st states that this issue would entirely replace the old on August 27. . . .

In October, 1862, the first branch postoffice was established at the northwest corner of Randolph and Halsted Streets and was known as West Branch. Soon after this, North Branch was established—both used the oval markings familiar to collectors of Chicago covers.

Carrier service was inaugurated in 1864 and covered the entire city which was divided into 35 carrier districts. In 1866 there were 50 carrier districts.

In 1865 Samuel D. Hoard became postmaster and he was followed by Thomas O. Osborne in July, 1866, and he in turn by Robert A. Gilmore in November, 1866. Francis T. Sherman was appointed in August, 1867, and Francis A. Eastman, in April, 1869. The latter was postmaster at the time of the great fire of 1871 in which the Federal Building was destroyed. Temporarily the postoffice was located in Burlington Hall, at State and 16th Streets (No. 8 on map), but on Christmas Day, 1871, moved into the Methodist Church at Harrison and Wabash (No. 9 on map), where it remained until burned out in the fire of 1874. During this period the government decided on a permanent location in the block bounded by Dearborn, Jackson, Clark and Adams Streets (No. 10 on map). This site after the completion of the building, served as postoffice and Federal building until the move which located the postoffice at VanBuren and Canal Streets, west of the Chicago river (No. 11 on map).

STAMPLESS COVERS

By the time Chicago opened its post office in 1831 many of the procedures for handling and marking the mail had been established. Henry Bishop had invented the postmark when he became head of the London General Post Office at the Restoration in 1660. The original design consisted of a circle divided into two compartments by a line with the abbreviated month in one part and the date of the month in the other. Sometime between 1760 and 1770 it was supplied to the General Post Office of New York and later to Boston. Around 1770, type-set town names came into use, and these were found in both straight-line types and with circular dates. The large circular postmark appears to have been used in 1800, and these were employed by the Chicago postmasters, in some form, until the Civil War.

CHICAGO POST OFFICE in the 1840's, vicinity Clark and Randolph Streets. Engraving by W. E. S. Trowbridge. Courtesy Chicago Historical Society.

13

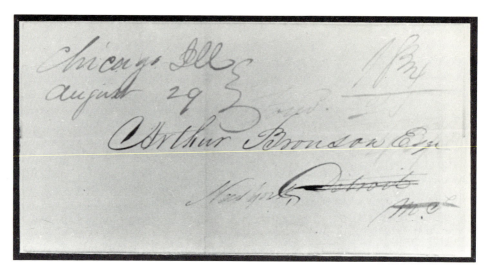

Red manuscript postmark with date "August 29" (1833), and with various red ms. rate markings. Letter, discussing current Indian affairs, was sent to Detroit, M.T., then forwarded to New York.

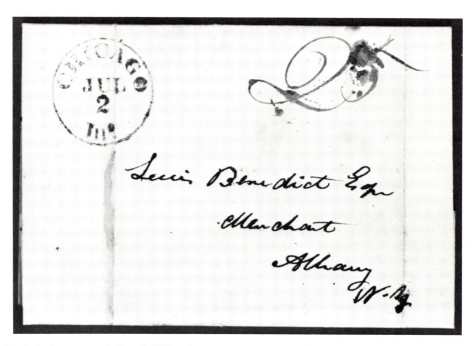

Red circle postmark dated JUL 2 (1833) with ms. rate. One of the earliest known postmark uses.

14

From the first mails despatched from Chicago in the stampless period until late in the 1850's, many interesting postal markings are to be found. Covers often had the place from which the letter was sent, the date, and the postage written in manuscript on the front of the letter. Later the large circular postmarks were used in company with a manuscript or a stamped "PAID." These postmarks are quite handsome and are found impressed in a variety of colors. Circles of different sizes were introduced, as well as letters of different thickness and style. These markings were applied over extended periods of time so that there is an overlap in their use.

One factor that influenced the makeup and character of Chicago postmarks was found in the requirements included in Acts of Congress establishing postal rates. The earliest applicable Chicago mail fees date from May 1, 1816, and, until 1845, were established on the basis of a single letter carried on a mileage zone basis. A "single" letter was defined as a single sheet of paper, and this was usually folded to a convenient size, usually 3-1/2 × 5-1/2 inches or less, and secured with sealing wax. Additional enclosures multiplied the rate, while letters weighing one ounce were charged a quadruple weight. Mileage was calculated along the mail route distances between post offices rather than by direct line.

The Act of April 9, 1816 (effective May 1) fixed the following rates:

Not over 30 miles	6¢
Over 30 to 80 miles	10¢
Over 80 to 150 miles	12-1/2¢
Over 150 to 400 miles	18-1/2¢
Over 400 miles	25¢

Effective May 1, 1825, the 150 to 400 miles zone rate was increased to 18-3/4¢ (1-1/2 shillings or bits).

The Act of March 3, 1845 (effective July 1) drastically reduced postal rates by providing that letters would be carried up to 300 miles for 5 cents, and for longer distances for 10 cents. The new rates are indicated on stampless covers of this period—and later on covers prepaid by stamps—by the numeral markings "5" and "10" in a small cogged or toothed oval. This law also provided that "every letter or parcel not exceeding one-half ounce in weight shall be deemed a single letter," thus permitting the use of envelopes and enclosures within this limit.

The Act of March 3, 1851 (effective July 1) established the following rates per one-half ounce:

Up to 3,000 miles	prepaid 3¢; not prepaid 5¢
Over 3,000 miles	prepaid 6¢; not prepaid 10¢.

The first stamps had been issued in 1847 to pay the 5¢ and the 10¢ rates but prepayment by postage stamps was not made compulsory at this time. The reduction in the prepaid rate was intended as an incentive to prepayment. In 1851, stamps were issued in 1¢ and 3¢ denominations. In many instances, however, letters were prepaid in cash and sent to their destination without stamps; the large round postmark with "3 PAID" at the bottom is found on such covers during the years 1852 to 1854. The same type occurs with "6 PAID," and also with the numeral "5" (for unpaid letters).

15

Black circle Springfield, Ill. postmark dated MAR 14 (1835) to G. S. Hubbard in Chicago. He added a note and remailed it to New York. Red circle Chicago postmark dated MAR 25, along with various ms. rate markings.

Red circle postmark dated OCT 26 (1836) with red handstamp "25" rate marking.

16

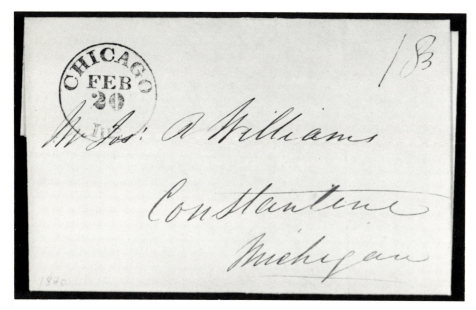

Black circle postmark dated FEB 20 (1840), with blue ms. rate marking "18-3/4."

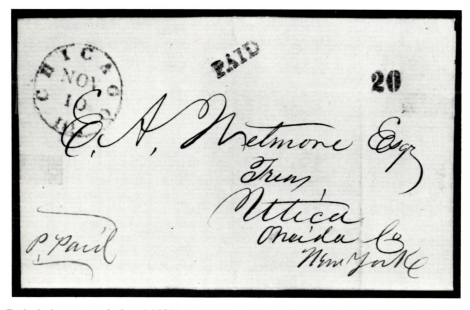

Red circle postmark dated NOV 10 (1840), with handstamped rate "20" and PAID in red.

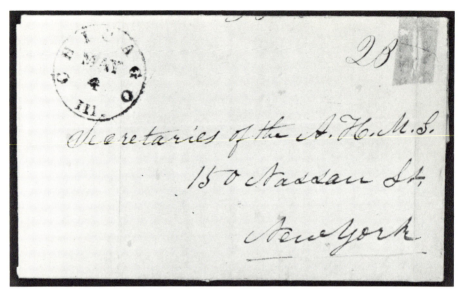

Magenta marking showing early use of this circle type postmark, dated MAY 4 (1843), with ms. rate "25."

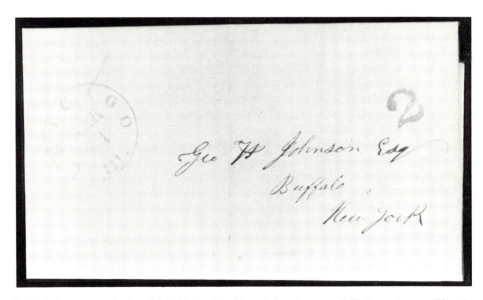

Red circle postmark dated MAR 31 (1846) and handstamped "2" on sheet calling for an Anti-slavery Convention for June 24, 1846, in Chicago. Example of rate marking per sheet of printed circular or advertisement.

Red circle postmark dated 28 JUL PAID 3 Cts. with red PAID (1851–1852 use).

Post Office Error—red circle postmark dated JAN 31 (1848 period) with strike-over of red "10" in cogged circle over red "5." Clerk may have used Lockport, Illinois, rate and then recognized the New York address and applied the proper rate stamp.

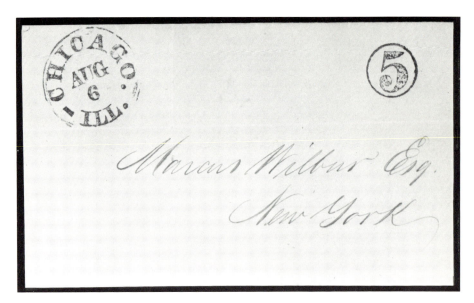

Red circle postmark dated AUG 6 (1851), with circled "5" rate marking.

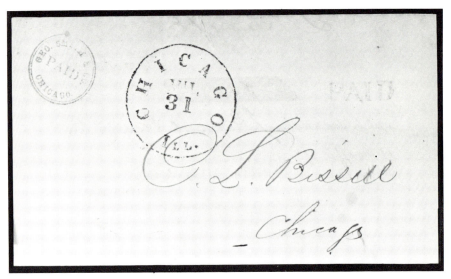

Black circle postmark dated JUL 31, with red PAID. Double circle of company sender PAID in blue.

20

Red circle postmark dated 30 SEP (1850), with red circle of rate "20."

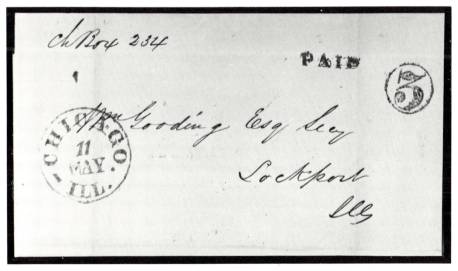

Red circle postmark dated 11 MAY (1852), with handstamped PAID and circled "3" rate. This rate marking was one of several types used in this period.

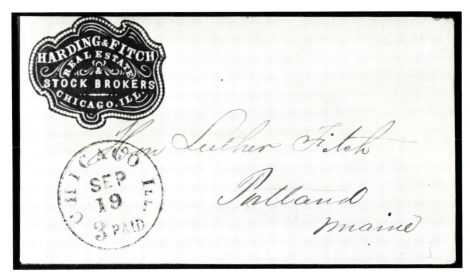

Blue circle postmark dated SEP 19 (1853) with "3 PAID".

Red circle postmark dated 16 DEC (1850) and unpaid red rate "40" on folded letter California, representing Pacific Coast rate 1847–1851. (California admitted to Union on September 9, 1850).

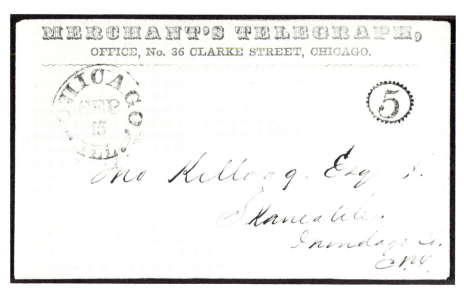

Red circle postmark dated SEP 15 (1851–1853 period) and black "5" in cogged circle on imprinted cover from MERCHANT'S TELEGRAPH.

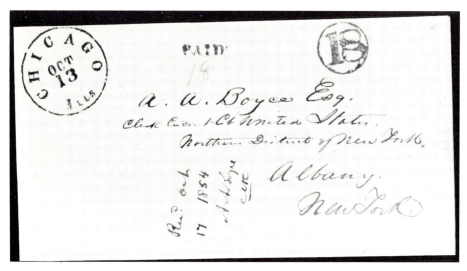

Black circle postmark dated OCT 13 (1854) with red PAID and circled "18"—six times single rate.

23

Black circle postmark used to pay circular rate with PAID 1 and dated MAR 3 (1855). Used on circular of the Illinois Central R.R. dated January 8, 1855.

Black circle year dated postmark NOV 2 1857, with black circled "1" for drop letter fee; ms. "Due 3" added.

Drop Letters, those handled entirely within the jurisdiction of a single post office, had been rated at 1¢, were raised to 2¢ in 1815, and then reduced to 1¢ again in 1851. They remained at this rate until 1863.

Cabeen reported (in *Stampless Covers*, June 1929) the following notation of the Chicago Post Office in 1852 to show that stampless and stamped letters went through together and that few letters actually were stamped:

> On Feb. 9, Mr. Wait, a clerk in the post office mailed one evening the following letters: Unpaid 3642; Paid and Distributed 6283; paid by stamps 280; paid in money 209; Free 471; Total 10,885.

It may be assumed that the item of 6283 was for purely local delivery letters and were distributed in the post office boxes; the item of 3642 includes all the unpaid, both local and outgoing.

The Act of March 3, 1855 (effective April 1) made prepayment on domestic letters (except drop letters) compulsory. The 3¢ rate per one-half ounce for distances less than 3,000 miles was continued, but a rate of 10¢ for over 3,000 miles was adopted, primarily for Pacific Coast points. The same Act also contained the following provision:

> From and after January 1, 1856, the Postmaster General may require postmasters to place postage stamps upon all prepaid letters upon which stamps may not have been placed by the writers.

This provision effectively marked the end of the largest category of unstamped covers. It must be stated, however, that compulsory prepayment by means of postage stamps or stamped envelopes did not then apply to local drop letters, circulars, or to foreign mail generally. These categories of mail, many of which continued for an extended period of time, represent some of the most interesting of stampless cover examples.

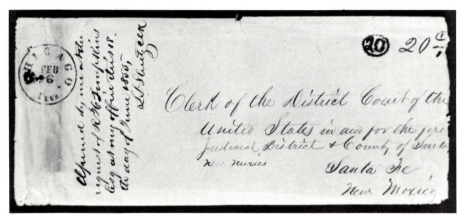

Black circle postmark dated FEB 16 (1855), with ms. rate "20." Red "10" in cogged circle inked over in black on double rated cover to New Mexico, Terr. Reverse signed by "I. Cook, PM" acknowledging receipt of letter Feb. 15, 1855. Registration of letters did not begin until July 1, 1855.

CHICAGO POSTMARKS USED ON STAMPLESS COVERS FOR DOMESTIC MAIL

Postmark	Data: dates seen—size—color—other markings
Chicago (ms.)	1833; (various ink colors and rates)
CHICAGO Ill^s.	"s" elevated. Thick letters 1833–40; 30c; Ms. rates; red or black
same	"s" elevated. Thick letters 1836–37; 29c; Ms. rates; red
same	same . . . 29-1/2c; magenta, red
same	"s" elevated. Thin letters 1838–40; 30c; Ms. rates; red, black or green
same	"s" elevated. Thin letters 1840–43; 29-1/2c; Ms. rates and "PAID"; blue, red (some without "PAID")
same	"s" elevated. Thin letters 1838–41; 30c; Ms. rates and "PAID"; red, green, blue
same	"s" elevated. Thin letters 1836–37; 30c; stamped rate (25); red
CHICAGO Ill.	1840–42; 28c; "PAID"; 20 stamped; red
same	1843–45; 29c; Ms. rates; red
same	1843–47; 29c; Ms. rates; "PAID"; red, blue, brown
same	1845–51; 29c; "5" & "10" in cogged oval; "PAID"; red or black
same	1845–46; "2" (circular rate); red
same	1851–52; 29c; "PAID 3" arc; red
same	same . . . black "FREE POST OFFICE BUSINESS"
CHICAGO.—ILL.	1849–53; 30c; red or black; "PAID"; red, blue or black "5" & "10" in cogged oval
same	1851–53; 30c; red or black; red "PAID 3" in arc; also "PAID" with 3 in 15c, 5 in 15c, 20 in 19c
same	1851–54; 30c; red; Ms. rates to foreign countries
same	same . . . "FREE POST OFFICE BUSINESS"
same	1849–50; 29c; red; "5" in cogged oval
CHICAGO ILLS	(LLS in ILLS smaller than I—break in circle over "I" in CHICAGO) 1853–55; 31c; red or black; with or without "PAID"; also some "5" (black) or "6" (red) in cogged oval
same	(circle complete and period after ILLS.) 1853–56; 32c; black; also red 16 or 19mm "PAID"; with or without rates

26

CHICAGO POSTMARKS USED ON STAMPLESS COVERS FOR DOMESTIC MAIL Continued

Postmark	Data: dates seen—size—color—other markings
CHICAGO ILLS.	(LLS in ILLS smaller than I, plus period) 1852–55; 31c with "3 PAID" in cds; red or black. Also "6 PAID"
same	same . . . 1853; 32c; red and black; also black cogged "5"
same	same . . . (without period after ILLS) 1854; 32c; red
CHICAGO ILL.	(LL of ILL smaller than I) 1855–56; 32c; blue or black; blue "5" cogged oval
same	same . . . 1853–57; 32c; "3 PAID" in cds; red, blue
CHICAGO ILL.	(10mm. between CH and ILL.) 1856–57 YD; 32c; black
same	(12mm. between CH and ILL.) 1856–57 YD; 32c; black
CHICAGO Ill.	(9-1/2 mm. between CH and Ill.) 1857–60 YD; 33c; black and blue
same	(11mm. between CH and Ill.) 1857–60 YD; 33c; black
CHICAGO Ills.	1860–62; 26 dc; Ms. or stamped "FREE"; "DUE 3"; blue or black
* *	* * * * * *
CHICAGO. ILL.	1855; 29c black, with "PAID 1" and date in cds (drop letter use)
No townmark	1846; 2 in red (circular use)
No townmark	1854; black "PAID" in large letters on 19mm. stamp (drop letter use)
No townmark	1853; black 39 × 20 oval "ADVERTISED NOV 1 1Ct"

NOTE: All measurements are in millimeters.
Edited material submitted to E. N. Sampson for revision *American Stampless Cover Catalog* (1970)

*Free Frank to Postmaster—Blue circle postmark dated DEC 4 (1840) and blue ms. "fr"
on folded letter addressed to Postmaster, Andover, Ill.*

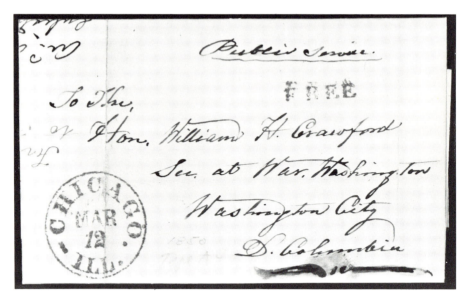

*Red circle postmark dated MAR 12 (1850) with red FREE and ms. "Public Service."
Letter addressed to William H. Crawford, Secretary of War.*

Red circle postmark dated SEP 17 with black handstamp "FREE POST OFFICE BUSINESS" and signature of postmaster "GEO. W. DOLE" (served as PM from Sept. 25, 1850 to March 22, 1853).

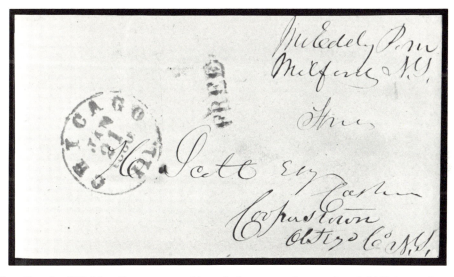

Free Frank of Visiting Postmaster—Blue circle postmark year dated JAN 21 1860, and blue handstamped FREE. Signature of Milford, N.Y. postmaster on cover to Coopers-town, N.Y. Scarce use of this postmark in blue or in use after December 1859.

*Free Frank to Member of Congress—Black double circle postmark dated AUG 13
(1860) and handstamped FREE, to J. S. Morrill, M.C., at Strafford, Vt.*

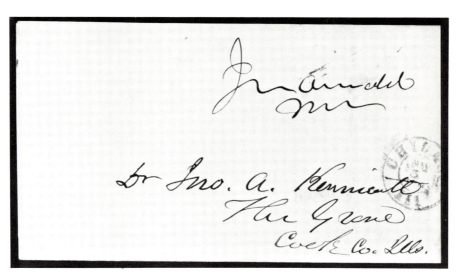

*Congressional Frank—Blue double circle postmark dated MAY 5 1862 below signature
of ISAAC ARNOLD, M.C. Career highlights of Arnold include: first Chicago city clerk,
1837; Member of Congress (Rep.) 1861–1865; Lincoln friend and author of* The Life of
Abraham Lincoln; *counsel for Mrs. Lincoln in her insanity hearing.*

1847 COVERS FROM CHICAGO*

When Chicago first established a post office in 1832 it was a hamlet of but 150 souls; by the time it was incorporated as a city in 1837, there were 4,170 residents. The continued influx of newcomers resulted in a population of 16,859 by 1847. Thus, by the time of issue of the 1847 postage stamps, Chicago had grown to a population of some 17,000 persons, and its gross area had expanded from one square mile to nearly 10 square miles. During the lifetime of this 1847 issue, 1847–1851, Chicago's population doubled.

Folded letter bearing NEW YORK POSTMASTER PROVISIONAL stamps addressed to Chicago jurist. New York red rated postmark dated 7 JAN (1846) with two initialled "ACM" pen-cancelled stamps on letter delivered to Chicago some 18 months before use of first U.S. stamps. The same Washington portrait, but facing to the right, was used by the engravers for the 10 cents U.S. stamp.

*Reprinted from *The Chronicle of the U.S. Classic Postal Issues* No. 59 (Aug. 1968), pp. 86–89. The author, Harvey M. Karlen, acknowledges his debt to the article by Richard Russell and George Wolters, "The 1847–1851 Postage Stamps in Illinois," *Illinois Postal History Society Bulletin* (Mar.–April, 1962), pp. 1–8, and to Creighton C. Hart, 1847 editor of *The Chronicle.*

Red circle postmark dated OCT 14 (inverted) plus red grid used to cancel 5 cents 1847 stamp; red "5" in cogged circle (1849? period).

Chicago was a city of young people, for of the estimated 34,000 persons residing in the area, half were children.

Although nearly all of Chicago's residents came from some other place, letter writing apparently was not as common as might be expected. One indication of this, we shall see, is in the number of stamps sent to the Chicago post office. Another indication is the limited availability of stampless covers from Chicago during this period. Since the sender had the choice of both prepaid postage stamps, or prepaid or unpaid stampless use, the need for using stamps was not important. Nevertheless, the issues of the *Illinois Postal History Society Bulletin,* 1955–1962, reported only some 30 stampless covers from Chicago during 1847–1851, one-third of which were 10¢ markings.

On December 1, 1847, John Marron, third assistant Postmaster General, reported that "stamps . . . have been issued to 95 postmasters for distribution. Notwithstanding they have been found very convenient in many localities, and under various circumstances, there has not been that great demand for them that was anticipated. Many important commercial towns have not applied for them, and in others they are only used in trifling amounts." Mr. Marron's remarks are tailor-made for Chicago. Chicago was one of the 95 post offices to receive an early supply of this first issue of stamps. The first shipment was sent on July 30 arriving on August 5, and consisted of 1,200 fives and 400 tens. Chicago was also one of the "important commercial" towns that used the stamps in "trifling amounts." The second supply of stamps was not requisitioned until nearly *two* years later when 1,000 fives and 500 tens were sent on June 8, 1849, arriving there on June 16. Commercial towns on the Great Lakes such as Detroit, Cleveland,

Red circle postmark dated 14 AUG (1850) with red grid used to cancel 5 cents 1847 stamp.

Red circle postmark dated 9 MAY (1851), with red grid used to cancel 5 cents 1847 stamp.

Red circle postmark dated OCT 20 (1847) with red grids used to cancel horizontal pair 5 cents 1847 stamps; red "10" in cogged circle.

and Chicago were just beginning their phenomenal growth during this period. Up until then seaports and river towns had been our large commercial centers.

Chicago, and the other 18 Illinois post offices that ultimately received shipments of the 1847 stamps, recorded a total of 28,300 of the five cent and 11,000 of the ten cent issue. The Chicago post office received almost half of the 1847 stamps sent to the state.

There are 44 covers listed bearing the 5¢ stamp, and nearly half of these are addressed to members of the law firm of Parks and Elwood of Joliet, Illinois, county seat of neighboring Will County. Other groups of covers include those in the correspondence of Anson Sperry of Marengo and of H. Mix of Oregon, both in nearby Illinois county seats, and all have to do with real estate transactions. There are eleven 10¢ covers reported from Chicago, and three of these are addressed to an officer of the United States Bank in Philadelphia.

Conspicuous on the accompanying lists are covers from the correspondence of the lawyer and land speculator, Dean Richmond of Batavia and Buffalo, New York. Ezra Cole, in a letter to the author, relates that Richmond supplied stamps of the 1847 series to his emissaries investigating commercial possibilities in Ohio, Indiana, and Illinois—including Chicago—and they reported their findings to him. Mr. Cole reports that two friends went through the old law office of Richmond and discovered between 50 and 100 covers bearing 1847 stamps, including ten or fewer Chicago covers. Of this number, he recalls handling a few pairs of the 5¢ and a single 10¢ on cover from Chicago. The numbered covers on the lists addressed to Buffalo are known examples from the Dean Richmond correspondence.

Most of these covers contain rate marks just as if they were stampless covers even though they all bear postage stamps indicating prepayment. The "5" or "10" Chicago rate mark is enclosed in a saw-toothed or cogged oval which usually did not hit the stamp. Covers with the rate mark within the saw-toothed cog used as an obliterator are popular and sell well, especially if the cog is clearly struck. On covers where the seven-bar enclosed circular grid is used as a canceller, the cog may also be struck well clear of the stamp. The cog is known on those covers indicated in the following tables, with the exception of those on which the townmark was used to cancel the stamp. Covers numbered 1 to 15 (and number 32) have the townmark with a circle 29 mm. wide and the state is indicated "Ill." This is a townmark in use from 1844 to December 1852, although no use has been seen on 1847 covers after December 1849, with the exception noted. Those covers numbered 16 to 35 have a later-type of circular townmark 30 mm. wide with a dash (-) before the state which is in capital letters "ILL." Both of these

5¢ 1847 STAMPS ON COVERS ORIGINATING FROM CHICAGO

No.	Date	Year	Cancel Color	Obliterator	Destination
			Singles		
1	SEP 3	1847	magenta	?	New York, N.Y.
2	SEP 3 (inv)	1847	red	grid	Joliet, Ill.
3	SEP 8	1847	red	grid	Joliet, Ill.
4	SEP 12	1847	red	cog	Joliet, Ill.
5	MAY 17	1849	pink	townmark	Rockford, Ill.
6	JUL 20	1849	red	townmark	Rockford, Ill.
7	SEP 28	1849	rust red	grid	Marengo, Ill.
8	NOV 18	1849	magenta	grid	Marengo, Ill.
9	NOV 20	1849	violet	grid	Monroe, Ill.
10	NOV 30	1849	magenta	grid	Marengo, Ill.
11	JAN 15	?	red	grid	?
12	JUN 30	1850	red	grid	Joliet, Ill.
13	OCT 14	?	red	cog	Joliet, Ill.
14	OCT 23	?	red	cog	?
15	10 FEB	1851	red	grid	Marengo, Ill.
16	DEC 19	1849	dark red	grid	Springfield, Ill.
17	DEC 13	1849	magenta	PAID & FREE	?
18	JUN 10	1850	dark red	grid	Kenosha, Wis.
19	JUN 18	1850	red	cog	Joliet, Ill.
20	AUG 1	1850	red	cog	Oregon, Ill.
21	AUG 14	1850	red	grid	Oregon, Ill.
22	SEP 14	1850	red	grid	Oregon, Ill.
23	OCT 1	1850	red orange	grid	Joliet, Ill.
24	DEC 18	1850	red orange	grid	Joliet, Ill.
25	DEC 31	1850	red	grid	Joliet, Ill.
26	JAN 7	1851	red	grid	?
27	7 JAN	1851	red	grid	Rockford, Ill.
28	JAN 10	1851	red	grid	Joliet, Ill.
29	15 FEB	1851	red	grid	Oregon, Ill.
30	MAR 6	1851	red	grid	Joliet, Ill.
31	APR 12	1851	red	grid	?

5¢ 1847 STAMPS ON COVERS ORIGINATING FROM CHICAGO
Continued

No.	Date	Year	Cancel Color	Obliterator	Destination
32	9 MAY	1851	red	grid	Rockford, Ill.
33	MAY 22	1851	red	grid	Joliet, Ill.
34	MAR 20	?	red	grid	Joliet, Ill.
35	MAR 23	?	red	cog	Joliet, Ill.
36	APR 7	?	?	?	?
37	MAY 2	?	red	cog	Joliet, Ill.
38	10 JUL	?	red	cog & PAID	Detroit, Mich.
39	DEC 11	?	magenta	grid	Joliet, Ill.
40	OCT 14 (inv)	1849	red	townmark & grid	Southport, W.T.
	h (horizontal)		*Pairs*		v (vertical)
1h	OCT 20	1847	red	grid	Buffalo, N.Y.
2h	NOV 13	1847	red	grid	New York, N.Y.
3h	DEC 8	1847	red	grid	Buffalo, N.Y.
4v	OCT 3	1849	magenta	grid	Buffalo, N.Y.
5h	OCT 3	1847	red	grid	New York, N.Y.
6h	13 FEB	1851	red	grid	Whiteboro, N.Y.

Red circle postmark dated SEP 21 (1849) with red grid used to cancel 10 cents 1847 stamp; red "10" in cogged circle.

36

postal markings were used on the covers or folded letters of the stampless and the adhesive stamp varieties of the period.

Similar markings are on the 10¢ covers. Those numbered 1 to 6 on the following list have the 29 mm. circular townmark; those numbered 7 through 11 have the 30 mm. townmark, each of course with appropriate type for the state designation as indicated above.

Noteworthy among the 5¢ covers is cover 35 which bears a copy of the extremely rare double transfer type "D." This cover was sold in a Newbury sale (1961) where it real-

10¢ 1847 STAMPS ON COVERS ORIGINATING FROM CHICAGO

No.	Date	Year	Cancel Color	Obliterator	Destination
1	NOV 23	1848	magenta	grid	Philadelphia, Pa.
2	SEP 21	1849	red	cog	Philadelphia, Pa.
3	NOV 5	1849	pink	cog	?
4	NOV 21	1849	magenta	cog	Philadelphia, Pa.
5	DEC 28	1849	red	grid	Philadelphia, Pa.
6	JAN 22	1850	red	townmark	New York, N.Y.
7	JAN 3	?	red	grid	Philadelphia, Pa.
8	AUG 30	?	red	grid	New York, N.Y.
9	OCT 1	?	pink	cog	Danielsonville, Ct.
10	DEC 2	?	red	cog	New York, N.Y.
11	?	?	red	grid	New York, N.Y.

Red circle postmark dated JAN 22 (1850) used to cancel 10 cents 1847 stamp.

37

ized $625 despite a "faint surface rub." Moreover, each cover bearing a pair of the 5¢ stamps is most unusual.

The shades of ink varied considerably as applied over the years by Chicago postal personnel for the various postal markings. Those shades have been described as "pink," which is pale, to a very dark shade called "magenta" or "maroon." "Chicago pink" is popular among collectors and the extremely fine 10¢ cover, number 9 on the 10¢ list, sold for $1,300 in a Robert A. Siegel auction (1961), the highest realization for any Chicago 1847 cover.

There are other known Chicago covers for which date of usage or other descriptive information is lacking. Each year also produces additional covers to supplement the lists in this article.

THE CHICAGO PERFORATION*

In 1857, when the United States officially issued postage stamps of the 15-gauge perforations produced on the Bemrose rotary machine by the contractors Toppan, Carpenter & Co., it was found that a number of postage stamps of the previous series had received unofficial perforations with their usage. These first stamps to appear in a perforated form are listed in Scott's *U.S. Specialized Catalogue* as follows:

(No.) 7 1¢ blue, type II, July 1, 1851
9 1¢ blue, type IV, June 8, 1852
11 3¢ dull red (1853–54–55), type I

Each of these items has a variety listing with "Perf. 12-1/2, unofficial."

Dr. Carroll Chase noted "numbers of well-authenticated stamps which show evidence of unofficial separation are known. Those which are most satisfactory were used in Chicago, mostly in the year 1856 . . . The perforation gauges very close to 12-1/2 although it varies slightly, rarely measuring nearly 13. . . . Well-authenticated copies of unofficial perforations are known from four other towns but none of them seemingly is in the same category with the Chicago perforations. . . ."

Copies of the 3¢ issue, on and off cover, appear occasionally today at auctions. Covers are known postmarked in the period from July 14, 1856, to January 22, 1857. A cover with a horizontal pair of the 3¢ bearing the January 22 cancellation (and signed by Ashbrook) was offered in a Robert Siegel sale #307 of January, 1970, and brought $1,050. The varieties of the 1¢, however, are extremely scarce. Stanley Ashbrook, writing in 1938, pays note of this scarcity:

> Chase stated he had seen some sixteen copies of the Three Cent and four copies of the One Cent Type IV. I have seen but one copy of the One Cent Type II. This stamp is from Plate Two, the 48R2 double transfer, and it is a single on a printed circular mailed from Chicago. Unfortunately there is no indication of the date of use . . . The circular is an advertisement of the "Lake View Water Cure, near Chicago, Ills," and has a wood cut illustrating this health resort. The stamp is on the regular paper used at that period (1856) for the imperforate stamps from Plate Two. It is cancelled with the black Chicago "PAID." . . . The "Chicago Perf" shows that in spite of the perforations, scissors (?) were used to separate the stamp.

The question of why these stamps were perforated, and who performed the task of perforating, has produced widespread controversy over the years. The authoritative

---

*A recent summary of the writings on the subject is found in the article compiled by Samuel Ray, "The Chicago Perforation," distributed by the Chicago Philatelic Society, *83rd Anniversary National Exhibition* (Nov. 7–9, 1969).

Black PAID on 1 cent 1851 stamp, Type II, Plate II, with CHICAGO PERFORA-TION. Used on Chicago Market Review and Price Current *dated 28 May 1856 to Canada.*

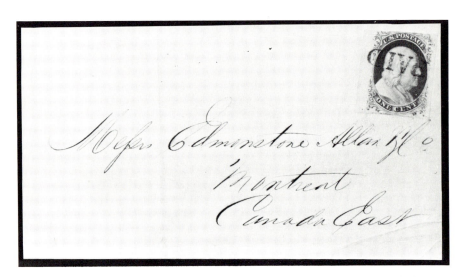

Black PAID on 1 cent 1851 stamp, Type II, with usage similar to that of Chicago Per-foration but a week later. On Chicago Market Review and Price Current *dated 4 June 1856 to Canada.*

Black circle year dated postmark SEP 12 1856 used to cancel 3 cents 1851 stamp with CHICAGO PERFORATION.

Black circle year dated postmark FEB 11 1857 used to cancel 3 cents 1851 stamp with CHICAGO PERFORATION.

word on the subject is probably found in various articles authored by Norton D. York. In *The American Philatelist* (May 1963), York provides the following explanation:

> It is the writer's opinion that this irregular 12-1/2 perforation *originated* in Chicago and at the *direction of the Postmaster himself.* He could have become irked at what he considered an unnecessary delay in the delivery of perforated postage stamps and decided to remedy the situation.
>
> This could have been accomplished there, because single-line stroke perforators, of the Henry Archer type, were in commercial use and the job could have been done easily, either at the office or in a city print shop.
>
> The so-called "Chicago Perforations" have been found postmarked from July 14, 1856, until Oct. 2, 1856, as near as the writer can ascertain, when they seem to have disappeared from use. Whether this was caused, after so short a period of time, by order or by an inadequate gauge of perforation, is subject to conjecture. At any rate, it is known that some were cut along the lines of perforations, apparently indicating that the paper was too strong for such a coarse gauge of 12-1/2.

While York may have erred on the dates of use, he does conclude that a study of the Bemrose patents indicates that the matching pins and holes were set to produce a 15-gauge perforation and were so used by the contractors until the 1857 stamps were displaced by the 1861 stamps and another contractor. Thus, it appears these Chicago perforations were purely local products, unquestionably privately made, (and similar to those used for receipt and check books,) and thought to be sold at the Chicago post office.

ADVERTISED MARKINGS

When Chicago postmaster Isaac Cook opened his post office on a new site in 1855 there were two windows made available for dealing with the public instead of the one window and a single clerk provided previously. For years the common complaint had been that patrons had been made to suffer long delays by standing in long lines outdoors to pick up their mail, or to transact any postal business. Despite this expanded facility, however, it proved inadequate as the volume of mail continued to overwhelm the post office staff. One newspaper reported that more than 400,000 locally mailed pieces per year had to be handled at this time. The average number of mails daily made up was 2,000, consisting of 250 bags, and containing 700 newspapers each. These were received and distributed daily.

Chicago's population in 1855 numbered about 80,000 persons with no mail distribution facility other than the personal pickup or sending someone to obtain it at the single city post office. There were no neighborhood pickup points to carry letters to the post office from the city's scattered homesites. The distance of some homes within the city limits to the post office was more than two and a half miles. It was not until 1864, with

Black oval marking ADVERTISED JUN 1 1 Ct., with black arc PAID 3, on cover originating from New Hampshire. Used in 1851 period.

43

the population grown to nearly 190,000 that the Post Office Department provided for a public carrier service. Chicago was a boom town with both a growing and a rapidly changing population, and the problem of mail distribution was a difficult one to resolve.

Post office advertising in local city directories of this period provides a clue to one aspect of mail distribution. These advertisements, reflecting the provisions of the Act of March 3, 1855, stated:

> Drop Letters for delivery only, one cent.

> Advertised letters are charged one cent in addition to the regular postage.

Regular advertisements, moreover, appeared in local daily newspapers favored by the postmaster (often his own paper), and they listed the names of persons to whom mail was addressed. Andreas' *History of Chicago* (1884) indicates the first "advertised list" appeared in *The Chicago Democrat* of January 7, 1834. It named one addressee. A year later the same newspaper listed 168 addressees. In the 1860's, lists appearing in *The Chicago Tribune* several times weekly each included from 1,300 to 1,500 names.

A wide variety of postal markings was used over the years to designate advertised mail and its handling. Oval, circular, and shield designs were favored until public carrier service was established in 1864. They were probably made locally as the shield marking, in particular, is notable only for its use in Chicago. Occasionally, covers are found with other stamped numbers representing dates the mail was claimed and the additional service charge collected, or the location number of the letter in the advertisement. Later, well into the Banknote period, undeliverable letters were advertised in the newspapers and a circular marking used commonly in many cities was applied to the letter.

Black circle year dated marking ADVERTISED FEB 1 1858, on cover from British Isles to Chicago, with black New York Exchange Office and British credit marks.

Blue shield ADVERTISED marking dated JUNE 20, 1860, with black double oval marking POST OFFICE DEPARTMENT DEAD LETTER OFFICE dated DEC 15 1860 on cover of Boston origin. Chicago backstamp dated OCT 1 indicates the Chicago post office held letter for three months.

Black circle marking "ADVERTISED JAN 1 1 cent," with black arc PAID 3, on cover of Indiana origin. Used in 1861 period.

Black circle marking ADVERTISED JUL 1 1 cent, on cover originating from Vermont, showing late use of 3 cents 1851 stamp. Used in 1861 period.

*Black shield ADVERTISED marking dated SEP 7 1861, on cover with 3 cents 1857
stamp originating from Detroit. Bears Detroit black oval STEAMBOAT DUE 2 CTS,
and red stamped "31."*

*Black shield ADVERTISED marking dated JUN 22 1863, on cover with 3 cents 1861
stamp originating from Wisconsin, and boxed NOT CALLED FOR.*

Chicago handling of cover from Wellington, Ill. dated JUL 12 1866, with 3 cents 1861 stamp pen cancelled: black SL "NOT TO BE ADVERTISED" and circled "RETURNED TO WRITER." Reverse has large circle CHICAGO ILL. JUL 18 P.M.

Black circle ADVERTISED marking dated OCT 24 and boxed NOT CALLED FOR on cover of Pennsylvania origin. Reverse has small circle receiving mark CHICAGO ILL. OCT 14 AM, with inclosure dated 1868.

CHICAGO POSTAL MARKINGS OF 1860 TO 1865*

Few traces of the city of Chicago of 1860 remain today except in the general layout of streets and waterways. Its limits had been fixed in 1853 and its area was only 17-1/2 square miles. Its length was six miles and its average width about three miles. The city reached from Fullerton Avenue on the north to 31st Street on the south, and from the lake to Western Avenue. Excluded from this was an area at the northwest corner, west

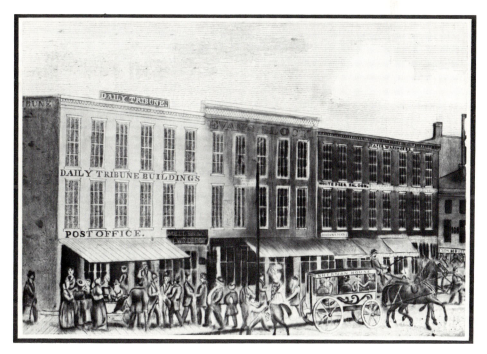

CHICAGO POST OFFICE in the 1850's. When a newspaper editor became postmaster, he usually established the post office close to the newspaper office. Courtesy Chicago Historical Society.

*Edited version of portions of article by Richard McP. Cabeen, "Chicago in August 1861," *Stamps* (August 5, 1961), and notes of a talk with this title presented before a local philatelic gathering in 1965.

Red circle postmark dated AUG 20 and black grid cancel on 3 cents 1851 stamp; black handstamp Hotel c.c.

Black circle postmark dated SEP 29 on 1 cent 1851 Type IV stamp to pay the circular rate.

Black circle postmark dated SEP 26 (1852), with 3 cents 1851 stamp tied by black "5" in cogged circle.

of the north branch of the Chicago River and north of North Avenue. Also excluded was a more extensive area at the southwest lying south of the south branch of the Chicago River and west of Halsted Street.

Chicago was not isolated but was closely surrounded by other communities of which more than sixty were annexed before 1893. Its population by census in 1860 was over 109,000 with an average monthly increase of about 1,000 persons. Transportation to the central area was provided by several independent horse car lines reaching the city limits at each side, but without through service.

In spite of its substantial population, Chicago's entire postal service was concentrated in a new federal building which had been opened in November, 1860, at the northwest corner of Monroe and Dearborn Streets. There was no letter box collection nor any carrier delivery and anyone who wanted to obtain his mail or to post a letter had to go to the post office or engage the facilities of Floyd's Penny Post.

The postmarks used in the period before 1860 were applied similarly to stampless covers or to the covers bearing stamps after 1847. (Ed. note: see section on STAMP-LESS COVERS) The postmark used in 1852 and 1853, for example, employed a much bolder type face than used for the previous types, and was first used in red, then blue, and still later in black. The state abbreviation was "ILL.," all caps with a period, and there was a heavy dash between the "C" of CHICAGO and the "I" of ILL. The word CHICAGO also was followed by a heavy period or stop. When used with stamps a black grid killer was generally on hand to deface the stamps, although the townmark also has been found to cancel stamps.

Year dates were introduced in the townmark used in 1856 and were included in the

51

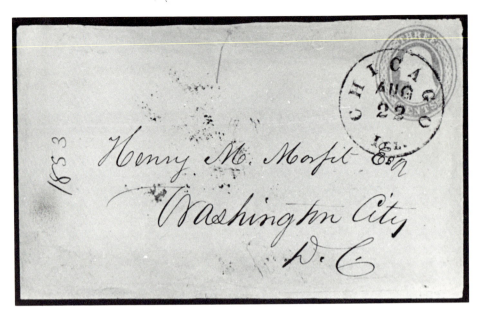

Blue circle postmark dated AUG 22 (1853) on 3 cents Nesbitt issue entire.

Black circle postmark year dated MAY 19 1856 on 3 cents entire. (10 mm. between CH—ILL). (Also found 12 mm. between CH—ILL.)

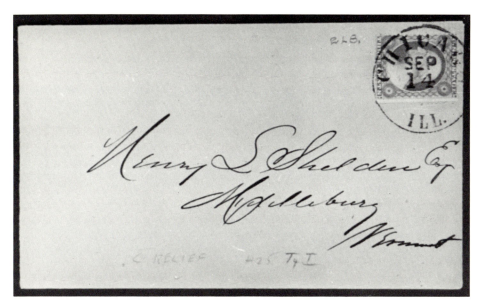

Black circle postmark dated SEP 14 (1857) ties 3 cents 1857 stamp. (12 mm. between CH—ILL). This marking represents very late use and is unusual for this period since it contains no year designation.

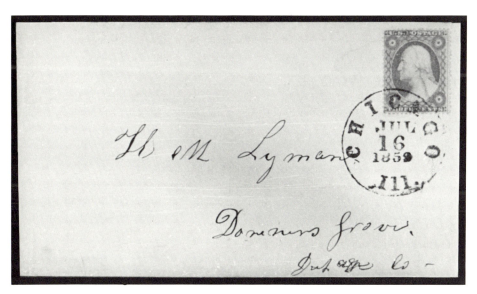

Black circle postmark year dated JUL 16 1859 ties 3 cents 1857 stamp. (9-1/2 mm. between CH—Ill.)

53

various handstamps employed to the middle of 1860, despite variations in the spacing of the letters of CHICAGO, and the different types of "ILL." and "Ill." (with and without a period after the final "L.")

The interesting period of Chicago postmarks starts with the introduction of a small double circle with month and day but no year. It is a duplex hammer with a grid to cancel the stamps. The state abbreviation is "Ills" in cap and lower case letters without a period. It appears in black or blue, at about the same time. The dates range from early in 1860 until July 9, at least, in 1862. This handstamp is found also without the killer attached and was used to postmark many covers. The handstamp was in current use when the 1857 issue was demonetized and exchanged in Chicago, August 27, and was continued in use with the 1861 issue.

A postmark quite similar to the preceding in size and design was introduced in the middle of 1862 but it shows a year date. It is also a duplex hammer with a target killer attached. In a great many cases it is impossible to read the year date, but it has been seen as early as July 12, 1862, in blue, and its use continues thus, with an occasional black impression, until about September 13, 1863. It has been mentioned as in use in 1864 but if this is so, some clerk must have found it in the discards. (Ed.: Norona does list this townmark in use to Oct. 21, 1864.) This postmark has been seen with covers bearing the Inspection mark applied to the letters of prisoners-of-war at Camp Douglas.

At about the 13th of September, 1863, the previous handstamps were discarded and an entirely new set placed in use. These also were a double ring type but of larger size and each bore a symbol in the form of a letter or two letters above the month and day date. There was no year indicated and the attached killer was a cut cork in nearly all cases. It seems to the writer that some kind of a test run was being made and that all letter mail postmarked in the city during the next two months bore one of the symbols. Then they vanished as quickly as they came. "RA" was in use at least from September 13 until November 3, but dates up to November 15 may be expected. September 13 which appears on one cover was a Sunday; November 15 also was a Sunday, but nine weeks later, not two months as might be expected for a test. (Ed.: for a fuller explanation of these initial markings, Camp Douglas, and Supplementary Mail cancellations, see the appropriate sections of this volume.)

The townmarks with symbols vanished as mysteriously as they came, and a new type was introduced about November 16, 1863. The design is identical with the former except that the symbol has been dropped and the two final figures of the year preceded by an apostrophe were added, but below the day date. The killer is a cut cork of varying designs attached to the townmark, and all like the preceding are in blue ink up to about November 18, 1864. Around this time there was a change from blue to black ink, and this change seems to presage the end of interesting postmarks in Chicago, at least for some years.

About February 1, 1865, the Chicago post office must have had a complete house-cleaning. The double circle postmarks were thrown out, and a nondescript small single ring townmark without year date was placed in use. It is a duplex canceler with cut cork attached and the entire mark is often barely legible. This basic townmark was to remain in use to about 1877, with variations in the size of the diameters of the circle ranging to less than 24 mm. to about 27 mm., and with differences in the spacing of the letters.

Chicago to California Via Ocean Mail—Black double circle postmark dated OCT 14 (1860) and grid cancel on 1857 stamps paying 10 cents rate; ms. "via Panama."

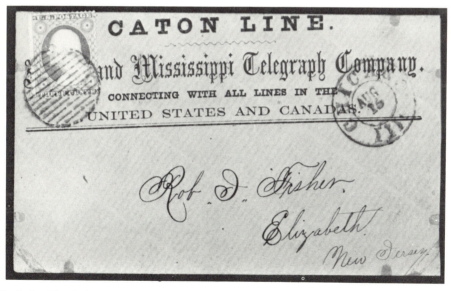

Black double circle postmark dated AUG 15 (1861) with detached 12-bar grid cancel on 3 cent 1857 stamp on Ill. and Mississippi Telegraph Company envelope. This grid cancel used only from September 1860 through August 1861.

Compound 3c plus 1c "star" die entire cancelled by double circle postmark with target attached dated JAN 26 1863. Used to pay local rate from Branch to Main post office in addition to the regular rate. Circle with directions believe applied by sender.

Subsidiary Marking applied by Chicago P.O.—Blue double circle postmark dated JUL 27 1863, and blue oval "Forwarded 3" on letter from Ypsilanti to Chicago and then forwarded to New Haven.

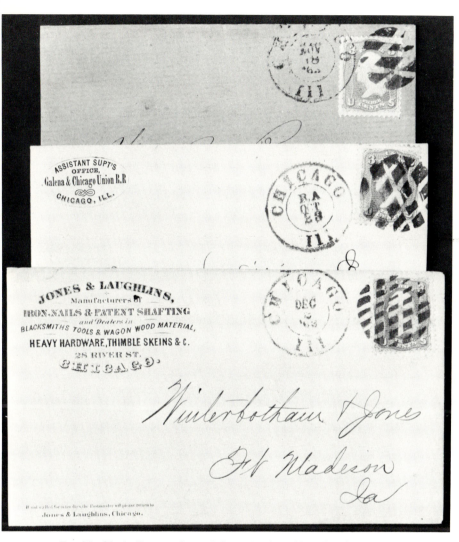

Double Circle Postmarks and Cancellations Used During 1863.

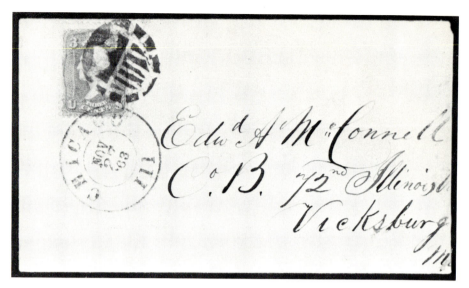

Blue double circle postmark year dated NOV 27 '63 and fancy (shield within broken circle) cancel ties 3 cents 1861 stamp. Letter addressed to soldier of 72nd Infantry, organized at Chicago as First Regiment of Chicago Board of Trade on August 23, 1862.

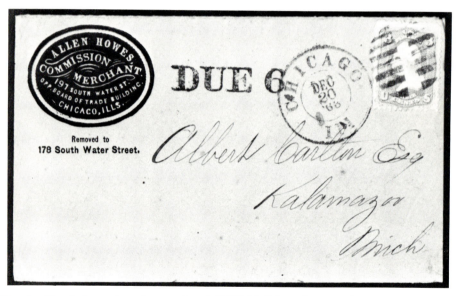

Blue double circle postmark year dated DEC 20 '63, and cut cork cancel ties 3 cents 1861 stamp; blue handstamp "DUE 6." Effective July 1, 1863, the law provided that in the event of improper prepayment, double the rate be collected on delivery. This letter was over 1/2 ounce and thus rated 6 cents due.

Double Circle Postmarks and Cancellations Used During 1864.

Black double circle postmark year dated JAN 9 '65 and cut cork cancel on 3 cents 1861 stamp. Represents late use of this postmark.

Black circle postmark dated OCT 2 (1865) and fancy (heart with US) cut cork cancel on 3 cents 1861 stamp. Such decorative killers were generally used in period 1865–1871, in contrast to larger fancy cancellations employed in 1870's.

FORT DEARBORN in 1857. Last remnant of Fort surrounded by growing city, from lithograph by E. B. Kellogg, printed by Rufus Blanchard, Chicago.

THE DEMONETIZATION OF STAMPS AND STAMPED ENVELOPES AT THE CHICAGO POST OFFICE DURING THE EARLY MONTHS OF THE CIVIL WAR*

The writer purposely speaks of this demonetizing at the Chicago post office, rather than calling it simply an exchange of new stamps for old, for it is possible that the office exceeded its authority in refusing to permit the use of old stamped envelopes which according to reputable authorities were never included in the ban.

A dispatch from Washington under date of July 16, 1861, reads in part, (as follows):

> The new stamped envelopes will be issued next. Facility will probably be given to holders of the old ones to exchange them within a limited time. The new stamps will not be issued before the first of August.

Although this dispatch is in no wise an official one, it is reasonable to assume that the reporter obtained his news at the Postoffice department. This appears to be the first word in *The Chicago Tribune* that new envelopes and stamps were to be issued.

Under a Washington date of August 12, 1861, the *Tribune* states:

> The new envelopes are now in the hands of the postmasters for sale. Some of them will carry 40, 24, 20 and 12 cents worth of mail matter, the larger denominations being adapted to the demands of the express companies.
>
> The new postage stamps will be ready for distribution at the last of this week.
>
> The recent Postoffice order providing against the transmission of envelopes with scurrilous matter printed or written on them, is not, as many soldiers and others suppose, to prevent the transmission by the mails of envelopes with patriotic or Union devices or designs.

---

*Many versions of this article by Richard McP. Cabeen are found; this was in *Stamps,* November 8, 1952.

In the August 14 issue a news item was captioned, "New Government Envelopes Important to Holders of Envelopes." It continued,

> As the public are aware the Government some time since decided to issue new styles of both government (prepaying) envelopes and postage stamps, in order to throw into disuse the old style of stamps held in large quantities by parties in the seceded states.
>
> By the advertisement in another column, it will be seen that the envelopes have been received at the Chicago Post Office, and are now ready for delivery to purchasers, and that the stamped envelopes of the former style will be received for postage or for exchange for the new envelopes prior to the 20th inst. after which date they cannot be recognized by the Postmaster, and will be consequently valueless.
>
> The designs are original and beautiful. The new stamps will probably be ready for delivery next week.

The advertisement referred to is a notice signed by J. L. Scripps, Postmaster, in which he gives the same information as above but includes mention of the "New Letter Sheets and Stamped Envelopes combined," something which escaped the eye of the reporter. From this particular mention of letter sheets it is apparent that these had never been on sale in the Chicago Post Office before that time.

On August 16 the reporter was shown the new stock and the items are described in some detail with the statement that those of the 6, 12, 20, 24 and 40 cent denominations are of the large size called "official" while those of the 1c, 3c, and 10c denominations

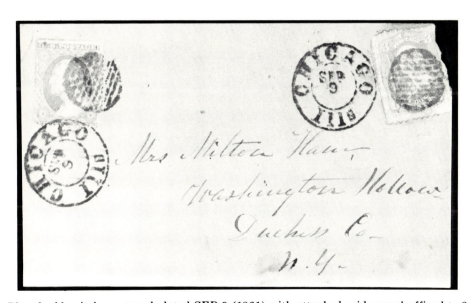

Blue double circle postmark dated SEP 9 (1861) with attached grid cancel affixed to 3 cents 1857 stamp and 3 cents 1861 stamp. Evidence indicates the valid stamp was added to the Demonetized Cover when letter was received at the post office.

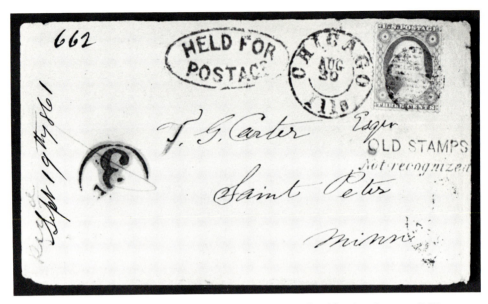

Blue double circle postmark dated AUG 30 (1861) and grid tying 3 cents 1857 stamp. This Demonetized Cover marked with black oval HELD FOR POSTAGE, a circled DUE 3, and OLD STAMPS NOT RECOGNIZED. Reverse has blue circle postmark dated SEP 9 and black oval DEAD LETTER OFFICE—P.O. DEPT. marking.

are in both note and letter sizes. He states that the stamps upon the 3c and 6c values are oval and show the denomination in plain figures on both sides.

He describes the higher values as having a rounder shaped stamp with a wreath surrounding the medallion, and with the denomination of all values given in plain numerals at the sides. No mention is made of the design of the 1-cent envelope, nor any description of the letter sheet.

On the same day the *Tribune* printed an excerpt from "Instructions to Postmasters," recently issued which reads:

> It being impossible to supply all offices with the new envelopes at once, you will deliver letters received from Kentucky, Missouri, Indiana, Illinois, Ohio, Maryland and Pennsylvania under cover of the old issue, until Sept. 10; those from the loyal states east of the Rocky mountains, until the 1st of October, and those from the states of California and Oregon, and from the Territories of New Mexico, Utah and Washington, until the 1st of November, 1861.

Following this item was another caution to readers to use or exchange their old envelopes before the close of post-office business on Monday the 19th, as they would have no value on the following day. Again on Monday the same notice to readers appeared, but then as today few read the paper and still less believed what they read.

On August 22, 1861, J. L. Scripps again advertised and this time it was to announce the new stamps. The notice captioned "NEW POSTAGE STAMPS" follows:

> The new postage stamps having been received at the Chicago Post Office, parties holding the old variety are hereby notified that the latter will not be recognized in prepayment of postage after the 27th inst., and that up to that time the new will be given in exchange for the old, if presented at the Chicago Post Office.

Two days later the *Tribune* commented that the change in envelopes and stamps had thrown a large amount of extra work on the postal employees "during the past two weeks as about 130,000 one and three cent stamps have been received for exchange and that nearly 50,000 stamped envelopes have been handled in the same time."

With the issue of August 25 the *Tribune* began a campaign to educate its readers who usually paid their subscriptions with unused stamps, mentioning that this "species of currency will become stump-tail on Wednesday, the 28th." The notice appeared in every issue until that date, involving not only the daily paper, but also a weekly and a semi-weekly edition.

On August 22 the post office published a list of stamped envelopes of the old style "held for postage" at the office. These are all identified by the name of the city to which they are addressed, and the writers of letters to those places are asked to come in and pay the postage. The first list consisted of six items, two addressed to Elgin, Ill., one to Rockford and three to LaCrosse, Wis. On each succeeding day new lists appeared, that of the 23rd showing twenty-nine items; and on the 24th, fourteen items; the 25th, fifteen; the 27th, nineteen; the 28th, ten; the 29th, nine.

It would appear that the absent-minded writers were learning as the list tapers off but not so; for on the following day the first list to include those letters bearing old stamps as well as those mailed in old envelopes appeared. On the date, the 30th, there were forty-one held; on the 31st, thirty-nine; on Sept. 1, thirty-seven; Sept. 3, thirty-six, and so on at about the same rate until Nov. 28, when the last list appeared. The dates missing in the list are for the Sundays on which the postoffice was closed.

This listing can be of some value in determining the validity of the Chicago marking "Old Stamps Not Recognized" for it appeared on each of those envelopes held for postage. The writer has checked several against the list and in every one examined there was a letter addressed to the town indicated on the cover, on the proper day.

During the period in question the *Chicago Tribune* was in receipt of more post office news than other Chicago papers and published the lists of advertised letters and what not. Whether the fact that the Hon. J. L. Scripps, Postmaster, was one of the owners of the *Tribune* had any bearing on the case is uncertain, or is it? He was appointed by Abraham Lincoln following the usual custom in which the Chicago postmaster was nearly always a newspaper publisher.

Blue double circle postmark dated JAN 3 (1862) with attached grid cancels 3 cents 1857 stamp. This Demonetized Cover is marked DUE 3.

Late example of Demonetized Cover handled by Chicago post office. Cover (and inclosure) from Garden Grove Iowa to New York, with postmark dated FEB 19 (1863) tied to 3 cents 1857 stamp. Blue double circle Chicago postmark on reverse dated MAR 2, with oval HELD FOR POSTAGE on flap.

THE PATRIOTIC RESPONSE
1861–1865

Illinois, along with other midwestern states, actively supported the Union cause despite the disaffection among the local Irish population. Chicago sent many companies and regiments into military service as soon as they could be recruited and trained. It was natural that expressions of patriotism would be common in the highly charged atmosphere leading to and during the Civil War and that these expressions would be found in all the then-known media of communication. Prominent and popular was the use of envelopes carrying a patriotic sentiment.

Campaign and propaganda covers were undoubtedly forerunners to the Civil War patriotic envelopes. They were first widely used in the presidential campaign of 1852 in which Franklin Pierce and William R. King of the Democratic Party opposed Winfield Scott and William A. Graham of the Whigs. Their use increased as the campaign of 1856 developed around the controversial anti-slavery and other issues with three political parties offering candidates. James Buchanan and John Breckenridge of the Demo-

Black circle postmark year dated APR 20 1858 ties 3 cents 1857 stamp on 1856 Fremont Campaign envelope.

67

Blue Double circle postmark dated JUN 25 (1860) cancels 3 cents 1857 stamp on Lincoln "The Railsplitter" Campaign envelope.

Blue Illinois town postmark dated NOV 2 (1860) ties 3 cents 1857 stamp on Lincoln Campaign Envelope. Lincoln portrait engraved by Ed. Mendel, 162 Lake St. Chicago.

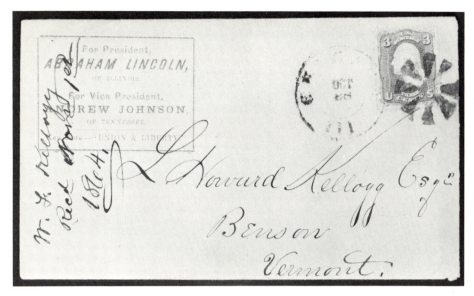

Blue double circle postmark year dated OCT 28 '64 and cancel on 3 cents 1861 stamp on Lincoln Campaign envelope. Front has Lincoln-Johnson advertising, and reverse has Union Party Platform reproduced.

crats, in a hotly contested campaign defeated Fremont and Dayton of the Republicans, and Fillmore and Donelson of the Know-Nothing Party.

The acrimonious campaign of 1860 brought to the fore the issues that eventually brought about secession. Now there were four tickets: Lincoln and Hamlin, Republican; Breckenridge and Lane, Southern Democratic; Douglas and Johnson, Northern Democratic; Bell and Everett, Constitutional Union. Patriotic envelopes made their appearance and they were used with passion in both the North and South. As illustrated in the catalog compiled by Robert Laurence of *The George Walcott Collection of Used Civil War Patriotic Covers* (1934), the envelopes carried portraits of generals, politicians, regiments, caricatures, some noble in sentiment and others hysterical. Perhaps the war years dulled the patriotic spirit as hardships and casualties mounted, for the use of such covers tapered off and they were less frequently used after the campaign of 1864.

Chicago was caught up in the fervor of the moment, especially in the aftermath of the death of the popular figure Colonel E. E. Ellsworth in Alexandria early in 1861. A long-time Chicago resident and organizer of the Chicago Zouaves drill unit, he was the first victim of a "southern" bullet. Many of the envelopes used in the first year of the war carried Ellsworth's likeness.

For the most part, envelopes were produced by eastern printers and lithographers, and Chicago printers and stationers often had their name imprinted below the stock designs. The variety was tremendous. The Chicago Historical Society reported on May 24, 1861, that it was in possession of more than 500 kinds of "Union envelopes," sent to it by publishers, stationers, and individuals, largely through the solicitation of a local printer. (Ed. note: this collection is still available for study.)

On August 2, 1861, the *Chicago Tribune* published the order to govern the delivery of soldiers' letters. Special provision was made for the mail of enlisted military personnel due largely to the inability of the troops to obtain postage stamps while in the field. Such letters were allowed to be carried without prepayment, but postage was to be collected from the addressee, providing the envelopes were endorsed "Soldier's Letter" and bore the signature of the major or acting major, with his regiment indicated by number and state. As indicated, this order did not apply to the letters of commissioned officers.

Yellow envelope with eagle patriotic design and matching stationery showing June 1861 use.

Multicolored printed flag on 3 cents "star" die entire showing 1862 use.

Chicago was filled with soldiers during this period. Military units from elsewhere in Illinois, from Wisconsin, Minnesota and other northwestern areas travelled through the city en route for service with the Army of the Tennessee in the Mississippi valley or the Army of the Potomac in the east. Some soldiers were returned to Chicago's camps for demobilization or re-enlistment when their short enlistment period was filled early in the war years. Most soldiers, however, were area recruits who were trained just outside the city limits, either at Camp Fry or Webb at Wright's Grove in Lake View at Clark Street north of the city, or at the southern end at 35th Street and the lake where Camp Fremont, and later Camp Douglas were located.

Closely related to the growth of the military services was the growth of allied welfare and medical services, often of an independent nature. The United States Government, while equipped to provide for a small national army during peace time, had made little provision to handle the needs of the sick and wounded of a greatly increased military force. On April 20, 1861, just eight days after the start of the Civil War, the Soldier's Aid Society was formed in Cleveland to assist in medical and welfare matters. Another company of women met in New York City on April 25 and organized the Women's Central Association of Relief.

These pioneering efforts led to the establishment of the United States Sanitary Commission by the War Department with the approval of President Lincoln on June 19, 1861, with orders for it to "direct its inquiries to the principles and practices connected with the inspection of recruits and enlisted men; to the sanitary condition of the volunteers; to the means of preserving and restoring the health, and of securing the general comfort and efficiency of the troops; to the proper provisions for cooks, nurses and hospitals; and other subjects of like nature." The Chicago office of the Sanitary Commission opened in October, 1861, and, as a fund-raising gesture, originated the idea

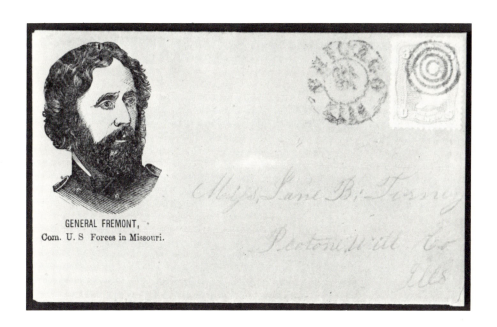

GENERAL FREMONT,
Com. U. S Forces in Missouri.

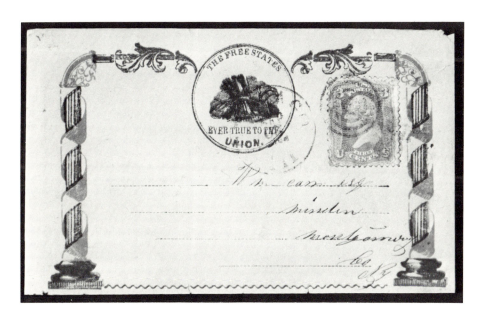

PATRIOTIC DESIGNS USED ON COVER WITH 1861 STAMPS

Patriotic Designs Used on Cover with Name of Chicago Printery—
D. B. Cooke & Co., 113 Lake Street.

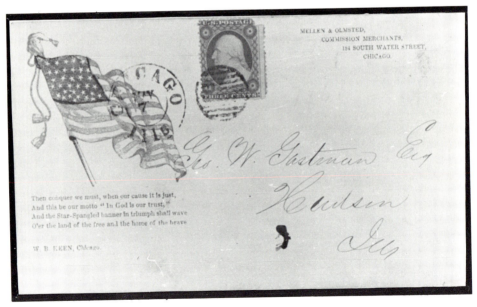

Patriotic Designs Used on Cover with Name of Chicago Printery—
W. B. Keen, 148 Lake Street.

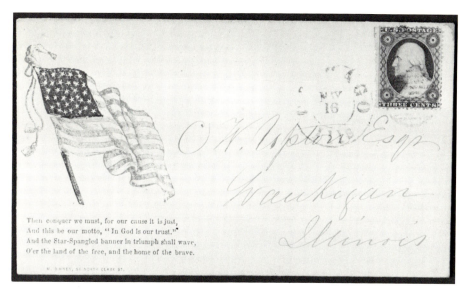

Patriotic Designs Used on Cover with Name of Chicago Printery—
M. Dinen, 54 N. Clark Street.

Patriotic Designs Used on Cover with Name of Chicago Printery—
Isaac A. Pool, 17 Clark Street.

Patriotic Designs Used on Cover with Name of Chicago Printery—
J. H. Johnson, 70 State Street.

Soldier's Letter—Blue double circle postmark dated JUN 14 (1862) with attached grid;
ms. "Soldier's Letter/C. W. David/Adjt. 51st Ill."; blue circled DUE 3. The 51st Infan-
try Regiment was organized at Chicago December 24, 1861.

Northwestern Fair advertising cover addressed outside of Chicago with black circle postmark dated MAY 8 (1865) and black cancel on 3 cents 1861 stamp.

of holding a large-scale Sanitary Fair. President Lincoln donated an original manuscript of the Emancipation Proclamation which sold at the Fair for $3,000 (and was later destroyed in the Chicago fire of 1871.) This combination of a patriotic and fund-raising device proved so successful that it was taken up by other large cities.

Unlike some of the fairs held in eastern cities, no special labels or stamps were issued by the Chicago Sanitary Commission. Special envelopes, however, were printed to be sold at the Northwestern Fair of the Sanitary Commission and Soldiers Home held in Chicago in 1865. These were printed in various colors with an advertisement of the Fair, and they contained a fancy shield of the U.S. Sanitary Commission. In addition, for this Fair, Charles Magnus of New York, issued a special illustrated cover called the "Union Rose" with a fan insert on which was printed a rose and views of Chicago and other northern cities. Old Abe, battle-veteran eagle mascot of the 8th Wisconsin Infantry Volunteers, was one of the attractions of the Fair.

Part of the effort in fund-raising and in providing soldier comfort was the assistance rendered by such other groups as the Christian Commission and the Soldiers Home. Their services included the provision of stationery, postage, and often the handling of mail for soldiers so that envelopes, letters, and markings associated with these organizations are represented in the postal examples of the period. The Chicago Sanitary Commission office closed in November, 1865, seven months after Lee's surrender. Andreas' *History of Chicago* reports that it spent an estimated $1,056,192 during the four years of its existence.

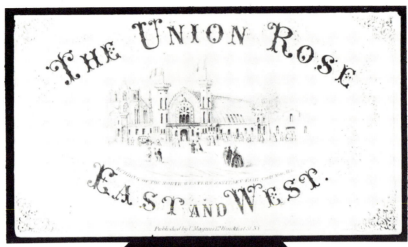

Magnus envelope "The Union Rose East and West" showing front with an illustration of Northwestern Sanitary Fair, Chicago, 1865. Inclosure is portion of the folded "Rose." Reverse has black circle postmark of NEW YORK dated FEB 8 (1865) to Andover, Ill., and considered the only known usage.

Blue double circle postmark dated X OCT 14 (1863) and blue cut cork cancel on 3 cents 1861 stamp on cover with CHICAGO SANITARY COMMISSION c.c.

Blue double circle postmark dated JUN 15 '64 and blue cut cork cancel on 3 cents 1861 stamp on U.S. CHRISTIAN COMMISSION c.c.

Military Mail to South—Blue double circle postmark dated JUN 4 1863 with target cancel on 3 cents 1861 stamp. C.C. of Chicago office of U.S. Mustering and Disbursing Office to 12th Illinois Infantry at Corinth, Miss. This site was captured by Grant's forces in May 1862, and was used thereafter as a mail distribution point.

CAMP DOUGLAS AND ITS CIVIL WAR LETTERS*

When it became evident that the southern states would go to war to preserve slavery—its greatest economic asset, Illinois and other states prepared to recruit and train soldiers. Chicago was made the recruiting center of the Northern District of Illinois and in September, 1861, Governor Richard Yates ordered a training camp to be established in this city.

The site chosen was just outside the south line of the city on the lake front and was a vacant level area which had served as an exposition ground two years before. This reached from Cottage Grove Avenue to State Street with its north line about 220 feet

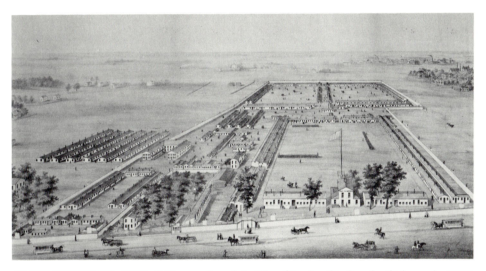

CAMP DOUGLAS, 1864. Lithograph printed by Charles Shober in Chicago in 1864. Courtesy Chicago Historical Society.

*Edited version of articles by Richard McP. Cabeen: "Camp Douglas and Its Prisoner of War Letters," *Seventeenth American Philatelic Congress Book* (1951); "Camp Douglas in 1862," *Ninth Midwest Postage Stamp and Coin Show* (1962), and also in *Stamps* (March 10, 1962).

Patriotic Cover Honoring Army Unit that Constructed Camp Douglas—Blue double circle postmark dated DEC 9 (1861) and grid cancel on 3 cents 1861 stamp. Envelope has imprinted SOLDIERS LETTER and MAJOR as well as portrait of COL. J. W. WILSON and unit designation.

south of 31st Street and south line at College Place (33rd Place) adjoined the building of old Chicago University.

The camp was named for the late Democratic Senator from Illinois, Stephen A. Douglas, and was on property which once had been a part of his estate. The camp site was about 750 feet west of the lake shore and had a ready access for troops to the Illinois Central Railroad which skirted the shore line at this point. It was served from the city by a horse car line from Lake Street along State and 22nd Streets and Cottage Grove Avenue to 31st Street. There was a little steam railroad also which ran between the site and Hyde Park, a populous suburb (to the south). This entire site is now covered by the buildings of the Lake Meadows housing development.

During construction (by the Mechanics Fusileers) the project was taken over by the federal government and was soon completed. The flag was raised at the parade ground on October 23 and for the next three months the camp was active with regiments training and departing for the front.

A rumor spread on February 4, 1862, that Camp Douglas might be converted to a prison camp for captured rebels, and this rumor changed to fact soon after the capture of Fort Donelson on February 14. Now the camp was rapidly emptied of its recruits and the first prisoners arrived February 17, 4,459 being listed on that and the following day. All were quartered in the regular company barracks around the parade ground and were guarded only by an occasional soldier under arms or a recruit with a club.

During April additional prisoners arrived, there being about 1,500 on the 14th taken at Island No. 10 on the 7th and on the 15th those from the Battle of Shiloh, April 10,

Prisoner of War Cover—Blue double circle postmark dated JUN 28 (1862) and grid cancel on 3 cents 1861 stamp. Ms. censor marking "Examined Bowen" and prisoner identification "From J. M. Rainey Prisoner of War."

began to arrive. On July 8 there were 7,807 prisoners on hand but they were soon to leave since a cartel for the exchange of prisoners-of-war was in the hands of the Secretary of War on July 23. This exchange got under way near the end of the month and by September 9 all were gone except one lone soldier listed as sick.

Now the camp again became a training center for recruits but this peaceful condition did not persist since by the end of the month it had been designated as a place for detainment for 8,000 Union soldiers captured and paroled on September 15, when the Confederate force took Harper's Ferry. These were in camp by the 1st of October and by October 3 were in a state of mutiny. When the terms of the exchange cartel were made known it was found that parolees could do nothing to advance the cause for which they had fought, until they were actually exchanged.

They could not be sent to the Indian frontier to relieve other soldiers and were sentenced to idleness. Had they been sent home to await exchange the chances of ever finding them again were remote indeed.

During the month of October the population of the camp increased to 16,000, a figure which included some 5,000 draftees in training. This far exceeded the capacity of the camp which became less livable each time the parolees decided to set fire to one of the barracks or the fence. It was a pleasant day for the commandant when an exchange finally released these men who were promptly shipped off to the front.

The year 1862 ended without a prisoner-of-war in camp but this condition was of short duration for during January 1863, prisoners began to arrive who had been taken at Murfreesboro, January 5, and at Arkansas Post, January 11.

Union Parollee Letter—Envelope with patriotic design and blue double circle postmark dated OCT 3 (1862) with target cancel on 3 cents 1861 stamp. Letter to soldier's sister in Vermont describes activities from capture at Harper's Ferry to Camp Douglas internment.

It is curious that there appears to be no example of a prisoner-of-war cover used during the 1862 period from February 17 to September 9. Undoubtedly many letters were written but perhaps they were not submitted for examination. The city was full of secessionist sympathizers who crowded the camp at first and may have carried out the letters. Lax supervision allowed many prisoners to spend evenings outside where letters could have been handed to chance acquaintances to post. Although there was much complaint about strict supervision, frequent inspections and the seizure of small personal belongings, the truth is found in the records which show that not until July 5 were five women discovered in camp who had arrived with the first prisoners from Fort Donelson. They were not camp followers but were the wives of soldiers who lived with their husbands inside the fort and who chose to don disguises and accompany their husbands into captivity.

With the arrival of "Morgan's Men" in 1863, correspondence really got under way for about four out of five covers now in collectors' hands are addressed to Kentucky. These covers and others to border states behind the Union lines needed no Confederate stamps to carry them to their destinations. They crossed the Ohio River at Louisville or at Cairo, and the Mississippi at St. Louis, and were promptly delivered wherever the United States post office was in operation.

Covers addressed to areas in the deep South or behind the Confederate lines, crossed only at designated places, and so far as this writer knows, only at the Fortress Monroe-City Point "Flag of Truce" meeting place, where Mr. Ould and Mr. Ludlow were wont to exchange their prisoners. The covers passing by "Flag of Truce" boats were taken to Richmond and then delivered to destination. The postage within the Confederacy could be prepaid with stamps or it could be collected in cash from the addressee.

Confederate Prisoners at Camp Douglas, 1864. Courtesy Chicago Historical Society.

The large oval "EXAMINED" hand stamp was impressed in black and less frequently in blue, until about the 1st of February, 1865. The mark is usually on the face of the cover. There is no indication whatever that the letter within the cover has been examined, that is, there are no initials or other marks. The covers do not show the return card of the writer, and it is just possible that this was not permitted.

The small round "EXAMINED" mark was used after about the 1st of February, 1865. It is always in black, and so far as can be determined, was used only with a small single line Chicago townmark which came into use only on February 1, 1865.

Covers within the camp period prior to about September 7 or 8, 1863, have a small double circle townmark with an attached grid or target killer, in blue or black depending on the dates. The grid killer went out of use in the summer of 1862 but the target is found as late as October, 1864.

The large double circle town mark came into use as early as September 8, 1863, and had an attached target killer for a very few days, then substituted a circular group of diamond shaped dots or lozenges. This on some handstamps at least was soon replaced by various "cut cork" types of killers. During all of the large double circle period two varieties are found: one with a space of 8 mm. between the "C" of CHICAGO and the "I" of Illinois; and a second in which the space is 11 mm. Blue postmarks were the rule until quite late in 1864. After November, 1864, only black has been noted.

The large double circle townmarks show the year date along with the month and day within the inner circle, thus "SEP/16/'64," in three lines, except for about two months beginning about September 12, 1863, and ending about November 13, 1863. During that period this writer believes that all Chicago townmarks whether for local mail or for out of town (or even foreign) delivery show a letter or letters instead of a year date. (See section titled *Chicago Double Circle and Local Postmarks with Initials* in this volume.)

Letter to Prisoner of War—From Simpsonville Ky. postmark dated NOV 15 (1862) with black Camp Douglas oval EXAMINED and ms. censor marking "C W Buttes Ex."
(Front only).

88

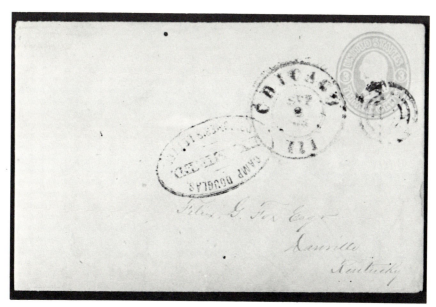

Prisoner of War Cover—Blue double circle postmark year dated SEP 3 '63 with attached target cancel on 3 cents entire. Black oval EXAMINED marking on envelope to Danville, Ky.

Prisoner of War Cover—Blue double circle postmark dated RA SEP 13 (1863) and blue cancel on 3 cents 1861 stamp. Black oval EXAMINED mark on envelope with patriotic design to Owensboro, Ky.

Prisoner of War Cover—Double circle postmark year dated DEC 15 '64 with attached cancel on 3 cents 1861 issue. Black circle RICHMOND postmark dated JA 17 on CSA 1863–64 10 cents Die A stamp. Black oval EXAMINED mark on envelope to Homewood, Miss., via Fortress Monroe despite ms. directions: "By flag of truce Via New Orleans La. and Mobile Ala."

Prisoner of War Cover—Double circle postmark year dated JUN 28 '64 with attached cancel on 3 cents 1861 stamp. Black oval EXAMINED mark on envelope to Rutherfordton, N.C. via Fortress Monroe. Faint Richmond postmark tied on pair 5 cents C.S.A. stamps.

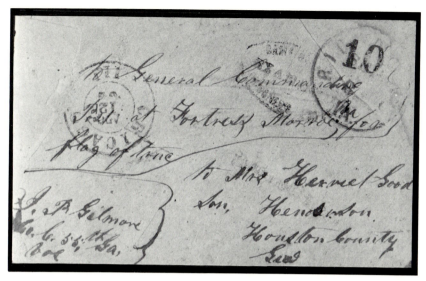

Prisoner of War Cover—Blue double circle postmark year dated AUG 12 '64; black oval EXAMINED mark on envelope to Henderson, Ga. Black circle RICHMOND postmark dated SEP 8 and black handstamp "10." Such mail, usually prepaid in cash, was enclosed in an outside envelope which was removed at Fortress Monroe and then carried to the exchange grounds; additional postal markings were then added, usually at Richmond.

Prisoner of War Cover—Black circle postmark dated FEB 5 (1865) and cancel on 3 cents 1861 stamp. Black circle EXAMINED mark on envelope to McMinnville, Tenn.

(Ed. note: Dietz states that another method of handling prisoner mail was also used. Letters were addressed to the Union commander as "General Commanding Post at Fortress Monroe, for flag of truce" as well as with the address and name of the party for whom the letter was intended. Such mail had United States postage prepaid in cash and such mail and coins for Confederate postage were enclosed in an outside envelope which was removed at Fortress Monroe and the letter was then carried to the exchange grounds. Additional postal markings were then added, usually at Richmond.)

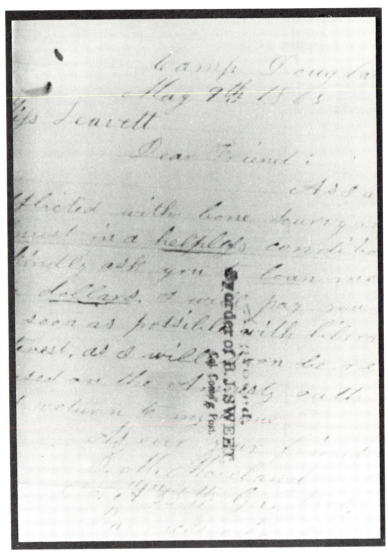

Prisoner of War Letter dated May 9, 1865, requesting financial assistance has hand-stamped censor marking "APPROVED/By order of B. J. SWEET/Col. Comd'g Post."

Prisoners were added following the various operations of Federal forces in the south in 1864. On September, there were 7,554 prisoners in camp. Additions brought the total on hand on December 31 to 11,702. From this time on only a few were added, many more being exchanged or released. The releases reached a peak in June, 1865, when 4,090 took the loyalty oath to the Union. By the end of the month no rebels remained in camp. On August 2, 1865, the Commissioner of Prisoners reported that Camp Douglas and its environs was vacated and "could be disposed of in the interest of the service."

CHICAGO DOUBLE CIRCLE AND LOCAL POSTMARKS WITH INITIALS*

The late Mr. Richard McP. Cabeen was best known for his work in the fields of territorial markings and of the 1851–57 stamps. He was interested in other areas, however, such as Chicago postmarks. One of the real puzzles in the latter field concerns the use of

CHICAGO POST OFFICE and CUSTOM HOUSE—Used from November 1860 until destroyed by Fire in 1871. Drawing by Louis Kurz, published by Jevne & Almini in Chicago in 1866. Courtesy Chicago Historical Society.

---

*Edited version of article prepared by Richard B. Graham that appeared in *The Chronicle of the U.S. Classic Postal Issues* No. 64 (November 1969), pp. 155–159, and based upon notes furnished by Richard McP. Cabeen. The tables have been revised and extended by the editor.

Blue double circle initial postmark dated RA OCT 1 with blue cut cork cancel on 3 cents 1861 stamp.

1863 Chicago postmarks with letters in the date logos slots. In *Chronicle No. 53* (October, 1966) a cover bearing one of these markings was reported and a request was made that covers with such similar markings be reported. . . .

This request brought a considerable response, which in turn aroused interest in further data which Mr. Cabeen requested. He also made a preliminary compilation of the reports received, which was sent in early 1967 to all who had reported covers. However, although several avenues were explored, no certain answer was found. The most probable explanation of the letters in these markings is that they are initials or other identification of the postal clerk applying the postmark. This is neither certain nor is a reason known. Although Mr. Cabeen's investigation developed an extensive record of covers with these markings, including such data as to where addressed, from what address the cover was sent (when available), the date of the marking, the killer which was duplexed with the marking and the owner of the cover, few real patterns are apparent from the compilation.

From Mr. Cabeen's notes we learn that this particular type of double circle postmark only came into use in Chicago a few days before the first postmarks with the letters appeared, his earliest recorded use being September 8, 1863. As the earliest recorded use of the letters in these town datestamps was September 11, 1863, these instruments were obviously new when the practice was begun.

For those not completely aware of how instruments with such markings are made, we should probably say that such handstampers were equipped with at least two slots and frequently, in this era, three slots into which date logos or special type could be inserted. If two lines only were used, then month and day, only, were shown; the third slot was for a year date. The normal arrangement produced a marking such as "SEP/10/'63" within the inner space of the double circle on three lines. When the let-

95

Blue double circle initial postmark dated X OCT 29 with blue cut cork cancel on two 2 cents Black Jack stamps (overpayment). Letter from Chicago attorney addressed to Alphonso Taft, Sec'y of War in Grant Cabinet and father of President W. H. Taft.

Blue double circle initial postmark dated GA SEP 19 with target cancel on 3 cents 1861 stamp, and with oval handstamp of NORTH BRANCH P.O.

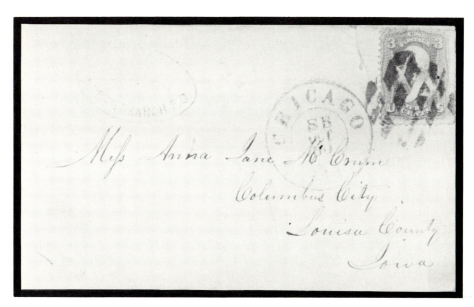

Blue double circle initial postmark dated SB OCT 30 with blue cut cork cancel on 3 cents 1861 stamp, and with oval handstamp of NORTH BRANCH P.O.

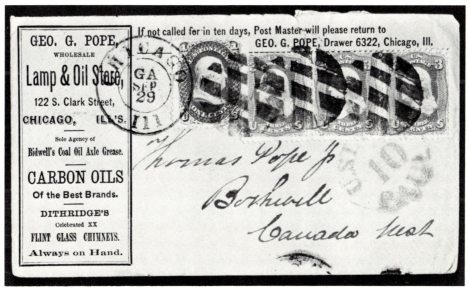

Blue double circle initial postmark dated GA SEP 29 to Canada, with 1861 issue stamps tied by blue cut cork cancel; red circle U. STATES PAID 10.

ters were added, the year date was abolished, the other two logos were moved down one slot and the "mystery" letters placed in the top slot. Four different letter combinations are known with the double circle marking. The two commonest are "RA" and "SB," but "X" is also well known. The last, "GA," is seldom seen, judging by the compilation.

In addition to the letters in the double circle marking, a similar practice was followed for roughly the same period for the local "CHICAGO CITY" single circle marking. Ten letter combinations, four being two-letter and the others each a single letter, are known with this marking. Mr. Cabeen had seen and examined all but one of the double letter combinations, which had been mentioned to him by the late Dr. C. W. Hennan. None of these markings is common; only three copies of "KB," two copies of "I," and single examples of the others were recorded. The marking not seen was reported as a "KM." We do not believe these local markings were accompanied by duplexed killers, but need verification of this idea.

Mr. Cabeen had recorded these for many years, but he was not aware of the earliest known date of usage, this having been reported after the list was compiled.

From the complete compilation, it may be seen that these markings were used, partially concurrently, from September 11, 1863 until November 30 of that year. Only a very careful study of the covers themselves would reveal just how many duplicate individual instruments were involved. We believe it was then the practice that each clerk in a large office might either have his own marking devices or at least that several such, intended to be alike, would be available. We would assume that the Chicago post office had several such double circle postmarking devices furnished, and it is possible that they were not all delivered at once, which might account for the staggered appearance of the lettered markings, although their disappearance from use is another matter. The use of the markings could apply to both location and to shift as well as to individuals. None of this reveals the reason for the use of the letters.

The fact that some of the markings, such as "RA" have more than one duplexed cork killer could indicate more than one instrument with these letters, but we prefer to think that the corks wore down quickly with heavy usage and were replaced.

Mr. Cabeen asked in his notes if double circles without the letters described were in use during the same period when the markings with the letters were used. He noted that Chicago carrier service did not begin until 1864, although there were West and North side branches established at this time . . . There is no connection between the street number arrangement of 1863 and those of today except possibly southward from 12th Street.

The purpose of collecting information as to where the letters were written was to determine if any geographic pattern of mailing was connected with the initials. Not enough data has been collected so that any conclusions can be drawn.

It was stated above that there may be a connection between the letter combinations and the initials of some of the post office personnel at this time. Mr. Cabeen gave the following names as being listed in Andreas' *Chicago,* Vol. III, page 601.

John L. Scripps, Postmaster	George B. Armstrong
Samuel Bangs	A. F. Bradley
Robert A. Gilmore	P. D. Leeward

Armstrong and Bangs were of Railway Mail Service fame. The letters underlined agree with certain of the letter combinations. Mr. Cabeen commented that some sources list Bang's name as George S. Bangs, although the listed version was probably correct.

CHICAGO CITY Postmark dated KB SEP 26 in blue, on 2 cents entire, indicating use of 2 cents rate to Bloomfield, Ind., for envelope carrying printed matter.

CHICAGO CITY Postmark dated KB OCT 13 in blue, on drop letter, with 2 cents Black Jack stamp tied by blue cut cork cancel.

99

CHICAGO CITY postmark dated I OCT 9 in blue, with 3 cents 1861 stamp (overpayment) tied by blue cancel, on drop letter. Envelope with stamp affixed in Natchez, Miss., was carried to Chicago and posted for local delivery.

CHICAGO CITY Postmark dated I OCT 19 in blue, with 3 cents 1861 stamp (overpayment) tied by blue cut cork cancel.

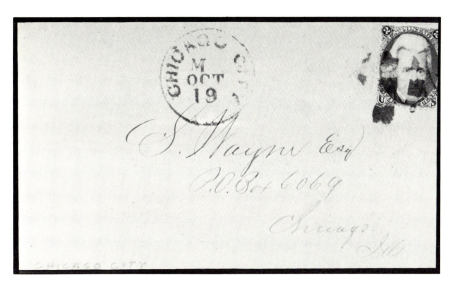

CHICAGO CITY Postmark dated M OCT 19 in blue, on drop letter, with 2 cents Black Jack stamp tied by blue cut cork cancel.

CHICAGO CITY Postmark dated OB SEP 5 in blue, on drop letter with large grid cancel on 1 cent adhesive and 1 cent "star" die envelope; blue handstamp "NOT TO BE ADVERTISED."

101

CHICAGO DOUBLE CIRCLE POSTMARKS WITH INITIALS

Letter	Date	Origin	Destination	Stamp
RA	9-11	Not given	North Enfield, N.H.	65
	9-11	Not given	54th Mass. Vols., Beaufort, S.C.	65
	9-13	Camp Douglas (1)	Owensboro, Ky.	?
	9-20	Not given	Newburgh, N.Y.	65
	9–23	Not given	Wells Corners, Vt.	65
	9-24	118 W. Lake St.	?	?
	9-25	Camp Douglas (1)	Cave City, Ky.	65
	9-27	Not given	Belmont, N.Y.	65
	9-29	Not given	Burlington, Iowa	65
	10-4	Not given	Mt. Sterling, Ky.	3¢ env.
	10-6	Briggs House, Randolph & Wells	Campville, N.Y.	65
	10-7	Not given	Hanover, N.H.	65
	10-9	Not given	N. Charleston, N.H.	3¢ env.
	10-9	J. Young Scammon	Boston, Mass.	3¢ env.
	10-11	Not given	Benson, Vt.	3¢ env.
	10-13	Chi. Commercial Adv.	Washington, D.C.	65
	10-14	Camp Douglas (1)	Louisville, Ky.	3¢ env.
	10-15	Not given	Three Rivers, Mich.	65
	10-16	Not given	Saline, Mich.	3¢ env.
	10-16	None given	Hopkinsville, Ky.	65
	10-16	Not given	Conway, Mass.	65
	10-17	Camp Douglas (1)	Louisville, Ky.	3¢ env.
	10-21	S. Cooles & Co.	Westchester, Conn.	3¢ env.
	10-25	Camp Douglas (1)	Cave City, Ky.	3¢ env.
	10-26	Not given	Campbell, Ky.	65
	10-26	Not given	Jonesville, Mich.	65
	10-29	Ass't Supt., Chi. & Galena R.R.	Woodstock, Vt.	65
	11-3	J. Young Scammon	Boston, Mass.	3¢ env.
	11-8	Not given	Jonesville, Mich.	65
	11-13	Not given	Angelica, N.Y.	65
	11-13	Camp Douglas (1)	Cave City, Ky.	3¢ env.
SB	9-21	Not given	St. Louis, Mo.	65
	9-22	Not given	Hastings, Minn.	65
	9-27	Not given	Milwaukee, Wis.	65
	9-27	Akers & Casey, 20 N. Lake St.	Washington, Ill.	73 & 65
	10-4	Webster, Marsh & Co. 67 Lake St.	Rock Island, Ill.	3¢ env.
	10-9	126 Dearborn St.	?	?
	10-12	Not given	Rock Island, Ill.	3¢ env.
	10-12	Not given	Milwaukie, Wis.	65
	10-16	182 N. Clark St.	Notre Dame, Ind.	65
	10-16	Not given	Morris, Ill.	pr.—65

Letter	Date	Origin	Destination	Stamp
	10-22	Not given	Washington, Ill.	65
	10-30	Not given (2)	?	?
	10-31	Not given	?	?
	10-31	Not given (2)	Rochester, N.Y.	65
	11-5	Not given	Warsaw, Ill.	65
	11-12	Lee & Antes, 121 Lake St.	?	?
X	9-24	Not given	?	?
	10-5	Not given	New York, N.Y.	65
	10-7	George Gardiner, Chi. Sanitary Com.	Lafayette, Ind.	3-65
	10-7	Rees & Slocum, 88 Dearborn St.	Hopkinsville, Ky.	65
	10-8	Not given	New York, N.Y.	65
	10-14	66 Madison St.	Climax Prairie, Mich.	65
	10-23	Not given	Hopkinsville, Ky.	65
	10-29	John A. Tyrell	Cincinnati, Ohio	2-73 (4)
	11-2	Gould & Bro., 159 S. Water St.	Logansport, Ind.	65
	11-3	Not given	Benson, Vt.	65
GA	9-14	Not given (2)	?	?
	9-29	Pope Oil Lamps, Clark St.	Canada	3-65, 61
	10-1	Not given	Burlington, Iowa	65
	10-7	G. A. Cook, Agt., Stomach Bitters	Washington, Ill.	65
	11-10	Not given (3)	Hutchinson, Minn.	pr.-65

Notes: (1)—with oval marking "EXAMINED" etc.
      (2)—oval West Branch post office marking
      (3)—oval North Branch post office marking
      (4)—overpaid

From the listings, it may be seen that some of the covers bear the oval "EXAMINED" marking of the Camp Douglas Federal prisoner-of-war camp where Confederate soldiers were confined, and other covers with the West or North branch post office oval markings. All these are struck on the covers in addition to the regular Chicago marking.

To speculate a bit, the fairly good fit of the initials of some of the post office clerks to the letter combinations is substantially indicative, if not conclusive. Consultation with the U.S. Register for 1863 might supply names of other Chicago postal clerks of 1863 whose initials fit some of the other letters or combinations.

If origin is unknown, there seems to be little point in recording more of these covers with "RA" or possibly "SB," except those which extend dates of use or have something else unusual about them.

CHICAGO CITY SINGLE CIRCLE POSTMARKS

Letter	Date	Origin	Destination	Stamp
KB	9-26	Not given	Bloomfield, Ind.	2¢ env.
	10-13	Not given	City—Gas Company	2¢
	10-17	Not given	City—Box 6069	2¢
KM	?	Noted by Hennan	?	?
OB	9-5	Not given—with SL "NOT TO BE ADVERTISED"	City	1¢ plus 1¢ env.
PB	10-17	Not given	City	2¢
B	11-30	Not given	City—199 W. Randolph	2¢
D	10-7	Not given	City—Box 6069	2¢
G	10-8	Not given	City	3¢
I	10-9	Not given	City—Box 1796	3¢
	10-19	Not given	City—Box 6069	3¢
M	10-19	Not given	City—Box 6069	2¢
O	10-17	Briggs House	City—Box 6069	2¢

CHICAGO SUPPLEMENTARY MAIL CANCELLATIONS

The Chicago post office is one of several known to have used "Supplementary Mail" cancellations, the others being Boston, New York, San Francisco, San Juan, and Honolulu. Dr. W. L. Babcock, who wrote extensively on the subject (See his 1939 pamphlet, *Supplementary Mail Markings*), could find no record of its sanction or origin for Chicago and had to depend on covers carrying the cancellation for his observations. Such markings were used from late 1859 to 1866. No evidence exists that these cancellations were ever officially sanctioned by the Post Office Department as was the case with the New York City supplementary mail cancellations, but the Chicago cancellations are recognized as specific "semi-official types, intended for a special postal purpose and comparable to the PAID, FREE, WAY, STEAMBOAT, CARRIER and RAILROAD cancellations of the times."

The term "Supplementary Mail" was defined in the U.S. Post Office 1879 Glossary of Words as "The mail sent at a supplementary dispatch," while "Supplementary Dispatch" was defined as "A special dispatch occasionally made after the regular dispatch."

Babcock's study of the then-known covers reveals that all letters receiving the Chicago Supplementary Mail cancellation originated locally. Arguments have developed as to whether it was used for a late bag of mail from the post office to the trains just before leaving, or whether it was used for a closed bag that was sealed for certain destinations such as Pittsburgh, Buffalo, etc. Cabeen provided one explanation in a note to Babcock (in *The American Philatelist,* February 1924) as follows:

> I can only offer an opinion regarding the "Chicago Supplementary Mail." I think that the Chicago P.O. as well as others probably sorted mail pretty thoroughly, as this was before the Railway Mail Service, or at least just as it was starting. I think none of the trains running east from Chicago were equipped at this date, 1865. All the mail for Pittsburgh was tied up in a package. Very likely there was sufficient mail for Pittsburgh, originating here and in the West, to make an entire pouch for that city. This would be sealed and marked so that it would not be necessary to look at the contents until its arrival at destination.
>
> Mail coming into the post office at Chicago after the pouch was closed, would be marked "supplementary mail" and forwarded to the next sorting office in a mixed pouch.
>
> I have no data on hand to attempt to prove this so can only say that it's a guess.

Some verification of this explanation is found in a Chicago post office notice printed in the *Chicago Press and Tribune* on January 23, 1860:

> Supplementary letter mails will be hereafter, made up in the evening only, for Toledo, Cleveland, Erie, Buffalo, Albany, Troy, New York, Boston, Detroit, Pittsburgh, Philadelphia, Baltimore, Washington City and all principal Eastern cities, thirty minutes after the advertised closing of the evening mails at this office.
>
> A supplementary letter mail will be made up at the same time for Cincinnati and the same arrangement will also extend to Canada.
>
> This arrangement will be continued irrespective of changes in the evening hours of departures of the railroad trains going East—provided that the advertised time of closing of the mails be prior to 6:30 p.m.
>
> Letters for the evening supplementary mails should be deposited in the chief clerk's room, No. 1 at the time indicated.
>
> I. Cook, P.M.

Apparently, the time for making up the mails varied with the season and the shift in railroad schedules from summer to winter. Post office notices before the railroad change date of November 4 for 1861 indicate the closing hours of mails at the post office for eastern railroads as 6 p.m. and 10 p.m. whereas the winter schedule from that date was 4:45 p.m. and 10 p.m. The Supplementary Mail notice in the *Tribune* on November 6 reads:

> For eastern cities (except Pittsburgh, Philadelphia, Baltimore and Washington City) and Canada close daily (except Saturday and Sunday) at 5:15 p.m. Letters (and letters only) must be deposited in the chief clerk's room (up stairs) after 4:45 p.m.

The evidence indicates that the fast east-bound trains (the forerunners of the New York Central lines) departed for eastern cities soon after the close of business, and the Chicago postmaster arranged to put letters only aboard those trains without extra charge. Since the Pittsburgh & Fort Wayne railroad (the forerunner of the Pennsylvania R.R. lines) had a fast mail train leaving at 10 p.m. throughout the year, there was no need to make similar arrangements for mail to cities along such routes. A few supplementary mail letters are known which were directed west or south of Chicago, but these must be considered accidental if identified as posted in 1861.

Two basic types of cancellations are known serving the function both of a postmark and a cancellation as no other obliterations appear on the envelopes. The impression was made by means of the usual type of metal hand stamps of the period. The earliest usages are of the large circular single-line postmark, 32-1/2 mm. in diameter, with CHICAGO at the top in large caps and SUPPLEMENTARY MAIL in small block caps below, and with the month date in the center. (This type is identified as CA) It is tied on stamps of the 1857 and the 1861 issues. The other cancellation is a double circle, 28 mm. in diameter, with CHICAGO and SUPPLEMENTARY MAIL between the circles, and the month date in the center. (This is identified as CB) While both cancellations were used concurrently, the latter is found only on the late printings of 1861. Both have been found in blue and black ink, although blue predominates for the former. Some variations in the spacing of the letters do exist. Since the month, date, and a cradle used

Supplementary Mail Type CA—dated JAN 10 (identified by Babcock with 1861 inclo-
sure), and blue grid cancel on 3 cents 1857 stamp. This is "the earliest known Chicago
Supplementary Mail" cover.

in the center of Type CB were interchangeable, as in the medium size double circle town mark with the attached grid killer applied to all other letters originating from Chicago, there are examples in which the cradle was replaced with the year (as 1862, or '64).

A study of the known covers with enclosures or receiving marks provides clues as to the year of use since, with few exceptions, no year marking is in the cancellation. The earliest known date of Type CA is January 10, 1861, and the latest—Type CB—is November 12, 1866. Few covers are known with stamps of denominations higher than 3¢ although there are known examples of the Chicago Supplementary Mail cancellation of 10, 12, and 24 cents off cover or on small pieces.

A number of scarce usages of these cancellations has been reported. A large commercial cover, addressed to Buffalo, has a neat Type CA struck on a block of four stamps of the 3¢ 1857 issue. An 1863 cover addressed to Baltimore has the Type CA marking along with the blue oval "North Branch P.O." A cover addressed to Belleville, Canada, has Type CA cancellation on three 3¢ and a single 1¢ 1861 stamps along with the red circular "U. STATES 10 PAID." The Type CA dated January 22, 1861, resting in a Chicago collection, is used on an embossed Lincoln 1860 campaign cover. Another collection has a Type CB used on a 3¢ envelope addressed to Kansas City, Missouri. Undoubtedly, the most unusual cover was the one stolen from the J. D. Baker collection. The cover, addressed to Boston, had a 3¢ 1857 stamp cancelled with the ordinary Chicago double circle dated June 13, 1862. A 3¢ 1861 stamp was cancelled with Type CA supplementary mail marking. In the flap, in clear view, was the straight line "OLD STAMPS NOT RECOGNIZED," and the oval "HELD FOR POSTAGE." Cabeen reported (in the *Chicago Tribune,* March 15, 1942) that no Chicago supplementary mail

Supplementary Mail Type CA—dated JUL 23 (1861), on 3 cents 1857 stamp. Example of late use of this marking applied to stamp of 1857–1861 period.

Supplementary Mail Type CA—dated JAN 26 on 3 cents entire with embossed c.c.

markings have been found on foreign mail although there "appears to be no good reason why some foreign letters should not have received this mark."

An attempt has been made to make current the known covers listed in the Babcock (1939) account. The list, while incomplete, may be considered fairly representative of the known values that were used and received Chicago Supplementary Mail markings.

CHICAGO SUPPLEMENTARY MAIL COVERS—TYPE CA

Stamp	Date		Color	Destination
1¢ 1857 Strip 3	Jul 15	(1861)	blue	Wooster, Ohio
3¢ 1857	Jan 10	(1861)	blue	Wooster, Ohio
	Mar 3	(1861)	blue	New York, N.Y.
	Aug 30	(1861)	blue	Bethel, Conn.
	Mar 14	not given	blue	Rochester, N.Y.
block 4	Mar 15	not given	blue	Buffalo, N.Y.
	Jul 2	not given	blue	Detroit, Mich.
	Jul 5	not given	blue	New Bedford, Mass.
	Jul 23	not given	blue	Lunenburg, Vt.
	Nov 2	not given	blk-gr	New Haven, Conn.
	Jan 22	(1861)	blue	?
3¢ 1861	Sep 13	(1861)	blue	Saratoga Springs, N.Y.
	Dec 6	(1861)	blue	Portland, Me.
	Dec 4	(1862)	blue	Cairo, Ill.
	Apr 19	(1864)	blue	New York, N.Y.
	Mar 25	(1862)	blue	Garnerville, Iowa
	Mar 31	not given	blue	New York, N.Y.
	Apr 2	not given	blue	Nantucket, Mass.
	May 31	not given	blue	Portland, Me.
	Aug 1	not given	blue	Galesburg, Ill.
	Sep 5	not given	blue	Salem, Mass.
	Sep 12	not given	blue	Logansport, Ind.
	Sep 15	not given	blue	Chester, Conn.
	Sep 29	not given	blue	Waterford, N.Y.
	Oct 24	not given	blue	Lowell, Mass.
	Oct 31	not given	blue	?
	Nov 6	not given	blue	Concord, N.H.
	Nov 17	not given patriotic	blue	Warren, R.I.
	Dec 14	not given	blue	New Haven, Conn.
3¢ env. 1861	Mar 10	not given	blue	Boston, Mass.
	Mar 25	not given	blue	Aurora, N.Y.
	Mar 27	not given	blue	Woodstock, Vt.

109

Stamp	Date		Color	Destination
	Apr 2	on piece	blue	?
	Jul 7	not given	blue	Madison, Wis.
	Sep 25	not given	blue	Galway, N.Y.
	Oct. 7	not given	blue	New York, N.Y.
	Oct 12	not given	blue	Akron, Ohio
1¢ 1861 & 2¢ 1863	Sep 29	(1863) with North Branch P.O. oval	blue	Baltimore, Md.
1¢ 1861-3		?	blue	Providence, R.I.
1¢ & 3-3¢ 1861	Sep 28	with c. U. STATES 10 PAID	?	Belleville, Canada
12¢ 1861	Jul 10	not given	blue	Wickliffe, Ohio

Supplementary Mail Type CA—dated SEP 29, on 1 cent 1861 and 2 cent Black Jack stamps; with blue oval NORTH BRANCH P.O.

Stamp	Date		Color	Destination
3¢ 1861	Aug 24	(1862)	black	Portland, Me.
	Jul 17	1865	blue	Detroit, Mich.
	Aug 9	1865	blue	off cover
	Aug 23	1865	?	New York, N.Y.
pair	Oct 30	'65	blue	Buffalo, N.Y.
	Dec 11	'65	blue	Chester, N.H.
	Jan 2	'66	black	Albany, N.Y.
	Nov 12	1866	black	Huron, Ohio
	Apr ?	not given	black	Boston, Mass.
	Apr 3	not given	black	Newburgh, N.Y.
	Jul 3	not given	black	Boston, Mass.
	Sep 9	not given	black	Cherry Valley, Mass.
	Oct 2	not given	black	Greenfield, Mass.
	Nov 12	not given	black	Akron, Ohio
	Nov 24	not given	black	Pittsburgh, Pa.
3¢ env.	Jan 12	not given	black	Rochester, N.Y.
1861	Oct 22	not given	black	Kansas City, Mo.
	Jul 3	(1866)	black	Boston, Mass.
3¢ 1861 & 3¢ env.	Sep 5	not given	black	Cherry Valley, Mass.
24¢ 1861	Jul 19	1865	blue	off cover

Supplementary Mail Type CB—dated SEP 10 plus cradle, cancels 3 cents 1861 stamp and 3 cents entire.

Supplementary Mail Type CB—dated JUL 3 with portion of 1866 in cradle, cancels 3 cents entire; also bears Chicago sender dated handstamp JUL 3 1866.

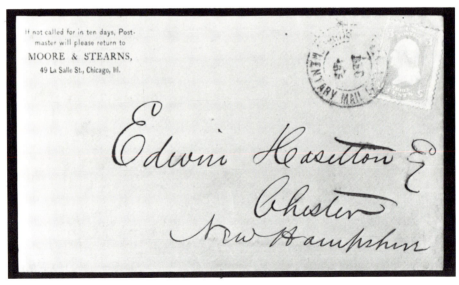

Supplementary Mail Type CB—dated DEC 1 '65 (no cradle) cancels 3 cents 1861 stamp.

INDEPENDENT MAILS, LOCAL POSTS, AND EXPRESS SERVICES ASSOCIATED WITH CHICAGO

INDEPENDENT MAIL ROUTES

The independent mail routes commenced operation shortly after 1840 and they lasted until forced out of business when the United States postage was reduced to 5 cents and 10 cents on a zone basis commencing July 1, 1845. Most of these private routes were in operation only a year or two and their charges were generally similar to or lower than those of the U.S. mails. Many of these companies issued stamps which served as an attractive label model for the post office department at a time when that agency did not issue postage stamps.

These independent mail firms had an important impact on United States postal history in many ways. Elliott Perry had this observation to make on them in *Pat Paragraphs* (No. 3, Aug.–Sept. 1931):

> Congress was compelled to reduce the government postage in 1845 because so many letters bearing the Hale & Co. or other independent mails, not only along the more thickly populated Atlantic seaboard, but as far west as Chicago. The U.S. stamps were issued in 5¢ and 10¢ to meet the rate charged by the American Mail Co., Hale & Co., Letter Express, Pomeroy & Co. and other independent routes whose stamps were usually sold at "twenty for a dollar."

Chicago established an express company connection with the east five years after becoming a city. Dr. Hennan writes that "Hawley & Co. operated an express service from Buffalo to Chicago in 1842" and "on April 3, 1843 Miller & Co., started the first tri-weekly express between Chicago and the east." Wells & Co. acquired the Miller interests and extended the Letter Express to Chicago about August 1, 1844, a mail route independent of the U.S. Post Office. Their local agents were S. F. Gale & Co., a book store at 106 Lake Street. This company which became the immense Wells-Fargo Express, especially after it expanded its business on the Pacific Coast after July, 1852, issued stamps of various denominations (*e.g.,* 20 for $1.00, etc.), with their $1.00 value featuring a seated figure "Commerce," later to prove popular as a model for stamps of other lands, and these stamps were used to prepay postal rates. Covers exist without the company stamp but bearing an 18 mm. circular postmark reading "WELLS & COS/EXPRESS MAIL/FROM CHICAGO" in three lines in the center of the circle. The Letter Express apparently ceased operation around October, 1844.

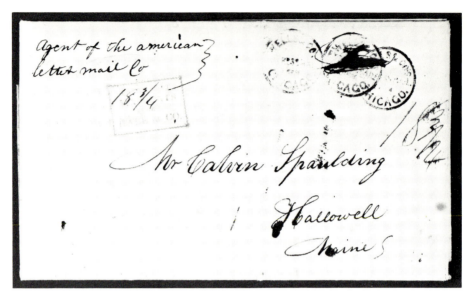

Independent Mail—Folded letter dated "Sabbath Morn, August 25, 1844" carried from Chicago to Buffalo by WELLS & CO (6-1/4¢) whose black circle handstamp is struck three times (for total postage noted in ms. of 18-3/4 cents); from Buffalo to Albany by POMEROY'S LETTER EXPRESS (6-1/4¢), and forwarded from Albany by HALE & CO (6-1/4¢); with red oval forwarding handstamp and red rectangular handstamp "COLLECT SIX CENTS."

LOCAL POSTS*

When the United States introduced cheap postal rates in 1851 it led to a heavy increase in the volume of mail and thus produced added confusion, delay and uncertainty in the handling of mail at post offices for both local and inter-city delivery. Some express companies had been organized earlier to carry letters and parcels between distant points and their number increased as transportation facilities improved. In many of the larger eastern cities, moreover, business firms were started to provide a local collection and delivery service for people living far from the post office.

Chicago was not far behind eastern cities in the introduction of these local posts but little is known about many of them except for a brief notation in a city directory. There is a note in the Proceedings of the Chicago City Council of February 6, 1855, of "The Petition of Peter Monter for the privilege of establishing a city dispatch post to deliver letters twice a day at two cents each." There is no evidence that anything came of this

*Material for this unit obtained from following sources: Cabeen, "Chicago Local Posts," *1000th Meeting of the Chicago Philatelic Society* (Oct. 4, 1928), pp. 13–18; Clarence Hennan, "Chicago: The Stamps and Mail Service of the Private Posts" *American Philatelist* (June, 1937), pp. 444–56 (also found in substantially the same form in *Second American Philatelic Congress,* Dec. 7 & 8, 1936, pp. 24–34); Henry E. Abt, "The Tale of One City: The Private Posts of Chicago" serialized in *American Philatelist,* June through October, 1957.

effort. Other listings prior to the financial panic of 1857 name three other private carrier services functioning in Chicago. The Stiles Union Despatch, 139 Lake Street, required pre-payment of its services in stamps in known denominations of five cents and twenty cents. Less is known of True & Thayer, 8 Dearborn Street, and Tobey & Clough, 94 Dearborn Street. Philatelists may yet turn up specimens of mail handled by these and other early firms.

Local Mail—Printed reminder of $1,000 note due Geo. Smith & Co. 11th March (1855 period) delivered and handstamped by black circle mark "McMILLAN'S POST DESPATCH." Only known example of this scarce marking.

McMillan's Despatch Post. William McMillan arrived in Chicago from Pennsylvania in 1849 and by November of 1853 was engaged as a druggist on Randolph Street. He is listed as a First Lieutenant of Company B, National Guards, organized in April, 1854. Andreas' *Chicago* states that in February, 1855, he established a penny post, the terms being one cent for each letter if prepaid; and two cents if collected on delivery.

Not much is known of this service. The *Tribune* of May 25, 1855, contained the following item:

> PENNY POST DELIVERY. We notice that McMillan is still industriously pursuing his well devised plan for a city dispatch by which letters and small packages can be carried to any portion of the city for the small sum of one cent. . . .

No other reference is found of this man and his post, and it is certain the enterprise was short-lived. Later city directories had McMillan employed as a clerk for the City Recorder (1856), and operating a drug store (1857). A single stamp is known and is illustrated in the Scott catalogue; it was typeset with an ornamental border, and the rectangle contains the name "McMillan's" and "DISPATCH" with no denomination. A black 18 mm. circular postmark was used on items of local delivery, with McMILLAN'S on top, POST curved at the bottom, and DESPATCH across the center.

BRONSON & *FORBES CITY EX-* *PRESS POST stamp* *cancelled by company* *circle.*	*MOODY'S DES-* *PATCH Stamp can-* *celled by blue com-* *pany circle dated OCT* *29 6 P.M. 1856.*	*WHITTELSEY' EX-* *PRESS Stamp can-* *celled by Company* *marking plus Chicago* *town marking (four* *copies known).*

Bronson and Forbes. Early in 1855, W. H. Bronson, formerly of Detroit, and G. F. Forbes, established the carrier firm of Bronson & Forbes at No. 5 Masonic Temple on Dearborn Street opposite the Post Office. Like McMillan, they offered two daily deliveries and two collections, but their rate, however, was two cents per letter. Bronson was believed to have been a printer by trade and the firm also handled books, periodicals and newspapers. Abt reports that a cover bearing a Bronson & Forbes stamp was pen-cancelled and dated March 21, 1855, as early usage, and that the latest known cover carried by the firm is January 7, 1857. It ceased to act as a carrier in the last quarter of 1857.

Two varieties of the stamps of this firm are known, the more common printed on green paper, the other on pale lilac. Central to the design is a head-on view of a locomotive, the source of Chicago's growth in the 1850's. The vignette is an oval 8-1/2 × 12-3/4 with a frame surrounding BRONSON & FORBES' CITY EXPRESS POST. Used copies of the stamp are known without cancellation, or with a circular mark containing the firm name and the date and hour.

Moody's Penny Dispatch. Robert J. Moody, formerly of Delaware, is listed in a city directory of 1856-57 as the proprietor of a City Mail and Express Post at 30 Dearborn Street. Started about January of 1856, Moody issued stamps for the prepayment of postage and charged only one cent per letter carried. The service lasted about a year. Abt reported the earliest known cover of January 5, 1856, and the latest November 4, 1856. The stamp is typeset, contains in three lines MOODY'S / Penny Dispatch / CHICAGO impressed on a vermilion-red glazed surfaced paper. Varieties may be found, particularly in the punctuation after the word "Dispatch." The cancellation,

116

Local Mail—BRONSON & FORBES stamp used on unpaid cover sent to Chicago and then FORWARDED by local addressee with city red circle postmark dated AUG 2 (1853 period) to Massachusetts.

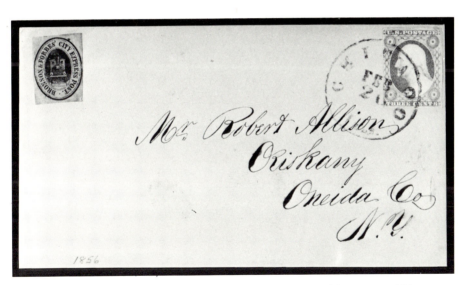

Local Mail—BRONSON & FORBES stamp used on cover with 3 cents 1851 stamp on letter picked up and carried to post office to enter the mails, dated FEB 26, 1856.

Local Mail—Valentine envelope probably delivered February 14, 1856, with red oval handstamp "MOODY'S DESPATCH PAID."

Local Mail—Red MOODY'S PENNY DESPATCH stamp cancelled by dated Company circle marking used on cover with 3 cents 1851 stamp tied by circle postmark dated SEP 16 1856.

used with either black or blue ink, contains the words "Moody's Dispatch," the month, hour, and year.

Whittelsey's Express. Edmund A. Whittelsey and Samuel M. Whittelsey, under the firm name Whittelsey & Co., conducted a short-lived City Dispatch Post from their offices in the Exchange Building at the corner of Lake and Clark Streets. They are found in the city directory for 1857–58, but not in any year following. The stamp is rough in appearance, and it contains a profile of Washington in an oval frame under the words "WHITTELSEYS EXPRESS," and the solid figure "2" above the word "CENTS." It was evidently impressed from a wood block in red. The post had a hand stamp of oval design within which on three lines are the words "WHITTELSEY'S LETTER EXPRESS," and was used with blue ink.

Local Mail—Blue FLOYD'S PENNY POST stamp cancelled by black company oval mark and used on cover with 3 cents 1857 stamp with double circle postmark dated MAR 25 (1860).

Floyd's Penny Post. John R. Floyd accompanied his parents to Chicago in 1849 and worked in the family hardware business until his father's death in 1857. He had associated himself with the organization of the National Guard Cadets in March, 1856, and when this group came under the leadership of Elmer E. Ellsworth in 1859, the name was changed to the Chicago Zouaves. The record is not clear but evidently Floyd became a full-time business manager of Zouave affairs some time after his father's death.

Floyd initiated his Chicago Penny Post in July, 1860, and it soon became the best organized privately operated carrier service in the city's history. Operating from offices at 124 Randolph Street, the business grew rapidly. He increased the number of carriers from 8 to 16 in six months so that by St. Valentine's Day of 1861, the *Tribune* reported

*Local Mail—Brown FLOYD'S PENNY POST stamp tied by small black company cir-
cle mark and used on cover with 3 cents 1857 stamp cancelled by large grid, with double circle postmark dated SEP 4 (1860).*

*Local Mail—Lincoln "Railsplitter" campaign envelope bearing brown FLOYD'S
PENNY POST stamp cancelled by black small Company circle marking and blue
double circle postmark dated SEP(?) 16 (1860) on 3 cents 1857 stamp.*

120

Local Mail—Green FLOYD'S PENNY POST stamp cancelled with large company circle marking for local delivery.

Local Mail—Black FLOYD'S PENNY POST circle marking on letter originating in St. Louis but carried from Chicago post office to local address; dated July 5 (1862).

that Floyd delivered about 15,000 messages on that day alone. By June, 1861, war had come, Ellsworth was dead, and, as a trained soldier, Floyd decided to serve the Union cause. He assisted the commandant at Camp Douglas for a time while running the Penny Post. On June 20, 1861, the *Tribune* carried an announcement that he had sold his interests to Charles Mappa, a member of the real estate firm of Mappa and Collins. They subsequently moved their offices to the same address as the Post. Floyd worked with the new owners during the balance of the year, although newspaper notices indicated that he served part of the time as a lieutenant and drillmaster at Camp Butler near Springfield.

Floyd was actively enrolled in the army on January 2, 1862, and was on active service until he was captured and paroled at Harper's Ferry, September 15, 1864. He resigned from the army, returned to Chicago, and went to work for the American Express Company. He served as cashier of the company from 1868 until his retirement in 1890.

The story of the Penny Post after January 1862 is clouded. Mappa apparently operated the company under the names of Floyd's Penny Post and Chicago Penny Post, using the names indiscriminately. A few months after he purchased the company, Mappa sold out to Kimball and Waterman with offices in the Methodist Church Block on the corner of Clark and Washington Streets. No information exists as to the operations of this private carrier service from this point.

Floyd's stamps were typographed in blue, brown, and green, and they carry a portrait that is supposed to be a likeness of Floyd. Cabeen, in his correspondence with Abt, was convinced, however, that the portrait was of Floyd's hero, Ellsworth. Several cancellations were used, one being a circle with rays in the center around which are the words "FLOYD'S PENNY POST"; a second is a double oval with "PENNY POST" in the center and "FLOYD'S / CHICAGO" within the two ovals. A third cancellation is a circle which has in three lines the words "FLOYD'S PENNY POST / CHICAGO." The business of the post was confined largely to the delivery of circulars, notices, etc., although a number of covers is known that combine Floyd's stamp with a 3 cents stamp of the 1857 issue.

Chicago Penny Post. Confusion over the use of this company name has added to the mystery of who was responsible for the issuance of the famous beehive stamps. Cabeen

CHICAGO PENNY POST Company cancel on Company stamp.

CHICAGO PENNY POST Company cancel on 3 cents 1861 stamp, dated DEC 12 1862.

noted a cancellation on such a stamp contained the words "CHICAGO PENNY POST, Edward T. Cooke, Supt." and his conclusion was that this Cooke succeeded Floyd as manager. Cooke, therefore, was in the employment of Mappa. Cabeen later found an announcement in the *Tribune* (October 18, 1862) which Abt reprinted as follows:

> THE CHICAGO PENNY POST. A new Penny Post has been established in this city by John Johnson and Joseph F. Coupe, the office of which is at 113 Randolph Street. The proprietors intend this to be the best and safest medium in the city for the transmission of letters. All the mail matter designed to be sent out of the city will be promptly conveyed to the General Post Office in time for the various mails. Boxes have been set up at nearly every business corner in the city and stamps can be procured at those places or at the general office in the Kingbury block.

While Abt could not find specific evidence of the issuance of such stamps by this company, he does conclude with the observation that "the 'Beehive stamp' *could* have been issued by Johnson & Coupe." Hennan located two covers bearing this stamp, one of which is associated with November, 1862, although no specific date was given. Leslie listed the stamp in his catalogue in 1863, and it was judged to have been used in 1862–63.

Local Mail—Orange brown CHICAGO PENNY POST "Beehive" stamp pen cancelled, and used on cover with 3 cents 1861 stamp (replaced) with double circle postmark dated JAN 22 (1862).

Brady & Co. Little is known of this company that supposedly operated in the 1861–64 era, except that there exists stamps and a known cover bearing one of the Brady stamps. Hennan noted that in 1860 a Mack S. Brady was a collection clerk for the U.S. Express Company in Chicago. Perhaps this firm operated locally as a successor to one of the firms that followed Floyd's enterprise, and it ceased operations with the

Local Mail—Valentine envelope believed to have been used in February 1864 with brown circle handstamp "BRONSON & FALLS EXPRESS PAID."

opening of branch post offices and carrier delivery in the city. The Scott catalogue pictures a lithographed stamp in deep violet as "BRADY & CO₅ CHICAGO PENNY POST," but it does warn that "The authenticity of this stamp has not yet been fully established." Dr. Hennan, nevertheless, after careful study, believed the stamp to be genuine "even tho proof is lacking."

Allen's City Dispatch. Edward R. Allen, one of the last to conduct a local post in Chicago, arrived in the city in July, 1881, and established his Allen's City Dispatch around October 1, 1882. Before long, Allen employed 33 persons operating from offices at 125 S. Clark Street. Allen advertised that he would deliver letters and other items within the city limits faster than the regular city mail carriers. Allen was arrested by the postal authorities and was convicted of violating statute 3982, by establishing a private post route in an area served by the U.S. post office department. Operations ceased after Allen's conviction on February 5, 1883. He remained in the delivery business and was manager of the Chicago Telephone Company's A.D.T. circular delivery service until 1884 when he operated an independent business as Allen's Circular Delivery until May, 1885, and then took the original name of Allen's City Despatch for his business after this date.

Allen issued private postage stamps which were affixed to each letter delivered by his carriers. The value of each stamp was one cent although the stamps bore no value marking. They were sold to Allen's customers at 75 cents per thousand, or at a different charge varying with the amount of business entrusted to him. With the termination of his business Allen sold his stamps cancelled to local stamp dealers. The cancellation

124

used was a rubber hand stamp, usually using red or violet ink. This hand stamp was an oval, date in the center with "ALLEN'S CITY DISPATCH" above and "125 CLARK STREET" at bottom. To the right of this cancellation, usually hitting the stamp, was an eagle with wings full spread.

Cabeen noted that covers bearing Allen stamps are not plentiful and that they bore dates between November 3, 1882, and February 5, 1883. Nearly a dozen of these known covers were addressed to the Empire Warehouse Company of Chicago. All stamps on these covers are either red on white, red on yellow, or brown-black on white, although stamps in other colors are known off cover.

Local Mail—Red on white ALLEN'S CITY DISPATCH tied by purple company oval and eagle dated NOV 28 1882.

EXPRESS COMPANIES

The expansion of railroad lines proved to be an incentive for the growth of express companies organized to provide national or regional services. Chicago, as a rail center, naturally reflected in this development. The Chicago city directory of 1861 lists a number of express lines, some of which had been operating since the 1840's. The names of these firms recognizable today included the following: Adams Express, American Express, United States Express, and the Overland, California and Pikes Peak Express Co. The corporate name of this last-mentioned company added Central later, in order to emphasize the merit of the central route to California over the southern route. These express companies affixed their own distinctive colored labels to letters and packages which they carried outside the mails. Letters were regularly carried from Chicago, especially when the contents of the envelopes required safe handling. It is not unusual to find the facilities of such express lines used to carry a letter from one U.S. government

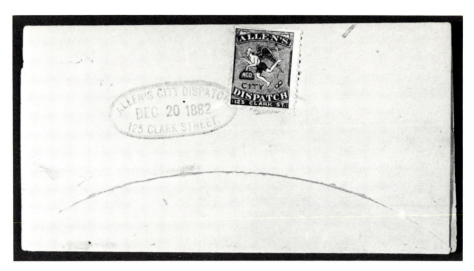

*Local Mail—Black on white ALLEN'S CITY DISPATCH tied by purple company oval
and eagle dated DEC 20 1882, used on wrapper.*

agency to the Washington, D.C. address of another rather than by the regular post
office mail.

Each express company also had its own seal which was impressed on the wafer or
blob of wax placed at the edges of the paper flaps. The seal usually contained the name

*Local Mail—Red on yellow ALLEN'S CITY DISPATCH stamp tied by purple com-
pany oval and eagle dated FEB 3 1883.*

126

or initials of the express line and occasionally included the name or number designation of the express office.

The operations of the Central Overland, California and Pikes Peak Express Company are associated with a dramatic chapter of U.S. postal history. It was this company that operated the Pony Express mail in 1860. W. H. Warden was the Chicago agent for the company, with offices in the McCormick building on the southeast corner of Randolph and Dearborn Streets. Wells, Fargo & Co. became the western agents of this company about April 1, 1861. The Pacific mail was assembled in their New York and Chicago offices or routed via Chicago over the C.B.&Q. R.R. to Quincy, then ferried over the Mississippi River. It was then taken across Missouri to St. Joseph on the Hannibal & St. Joe line (which later became part of the Burlington system), and then, when properly designated, carried by rider and pony to its California destination.

The first railway mail car wherein a crew of post office clerks "worked" the mail picked up en-route was run over the Hannibal & St. Joe R.R. in 1862. This mail sorting prevented delays at the Missouri River terminal and permitted the mail to be put on the Overland stage coaches as soon as the railroad train arrived at St. Joseph. Previous to the introduction of this system a delay for any cause meant that the transcontinental mail would lay over for perhaps a week at St. Joseph until the next stage departed.

Pony Express Mail—Chicago double circle postmark dated MAR 25 (1861) with grid on 3 cents 1857 stamp which carries letter to St. Joseph, Mo.; green oval marking OVER-LAND & PIKES PEAK EXP. CO. ST. JOSEPH, MO. dated MAR 28 indicates carried via Pony Express to Mountain City, Kansas T.

127

American Express Company c.c. printed on 3 cents entire and used on forwarded letter from Chicago with city double circle postmark dated DEC 12 '64.

Government Letter Carried by Private Express—"OFFICIAL BUSINESS" envelope of "CUSTOM HOUSE, CHICAGO" to Washington, with green label of UNITED STATES EXPRESS CO. and orange label of ADAMS EXPRESS; also with ms. "Free—H D Colvin" and blue crayon "DH", probably "Dead Head" with no charge made. Colvin managed U.S. Express Co. office 1854–1891, and was mayor of Chicago from 1873–1876.

CHICAGO AND POSTAL
WATERWAYS MAIL MARKINGS

Chicago's destiny has always been linked to its site located on strategic waters. Nature had created an inland sea, Lake Michigan, and a continental divide some eight miles from the lake's edge. From this divide the Des Plaines River ran southwest to the Illinois River and so to the Mississippi. Eastward to Lake Michigan ran the Chicago River in two branches that joined a mile from the beach. A narrow bog or portage separated the south branch of the Chicago River and the Des Plaines. The construction of Fort Dearborn in August of 1803 at the mouth of the Chicago River introduced ship traffic to the area as Captain John Whistler, fort commandant, guided the provision ship *Tracy* to the site.

The eastern mail was brought to the meager settlements in Illinois and Wisconsin twice a year, by foot overland in winter, and by boat in summer. Describing this activity in the period about 1825, the historian J. S. Currey writes in *Chicago, Its History and Its Builders* (1912):

> . . . The United States mails coming from the east to Chicago and other western lake ports were conveyed, during the season of navigation, by the irregular and tardy conveyances of sail vessels, and the inhabitants of the country were oftentimes for weeks or months without intelligence of what was passing in other parts of the world, from which they were completely isolated.

Little was done to improve water-borne commerce and the mails until later. President James Madison, in 1814, named Chicago's site as the northern terminus of the ship canal which he asked Congress to build through the DesPlaines and Illinois Rivers so that lake traffic might sail to the Mississippi without having to make the portage. It was not until August 4, 1830, however, that the commissioners of the Illinois and Michigan Canal laid the site out as a town in a survey and even named the principal streets of Chicago. Upon the advice of a young army engineer Jefferson Davis, Congress appropriated $25,000 in 1833 to clean the mouth of the Chicago River and erect a thousand-foot pier. On July 12, 1834, the schooner *Illinois* got over the sand bar which had been lowered by a timely river-flood, and Chicago's harbor life began. That same summer the steamboat *Uncle Sam* made a weekly trip between Chicago and Buffalo, while the steamboat *Buffalo* plied regularly between Chicago and St. Joseph, Michigan. Two years later work on the long-discussed canal was inaugurated.

Despite depressions and booms, Chicago's water-borne commerce established a firm hold early and continued to grow. In 1838, for example, 38 bags of wheat were shipped

129

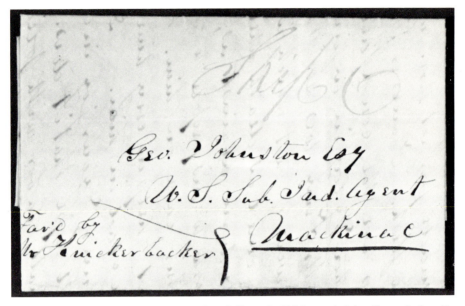

Ship Marking—Letter from Chicago dated June 6, 1834, carried by Great Lakes Boat to Mackinac and marked with ms. "SHIP 6."

on an east-bound boat, and 127 steamboats with 241 lesser vessels had called into the city in that year. More than 210 bushels of grain were shipped in 1841, and in the year following, 586,907. Immigrants from Europe and northeastern United States followed the water route by going along the Erie Canal to Buffalo and then taking a steamer to Chicago. This traffic was reflected in the postal practices current in this period.

A number of covers associated with Chicago's past bear markings related to waterway activity, the most common being Steamboat or Steam. A digest of postal laws relating to Steam or Steamboat markings on domestic waterways mail reveals that these markings are always an origin mark. This means that the letter reached the post office by means of a ship having no mail-carrying status and the marking was applied along with the postmark and canceller when the letter entered the mails. The Postal Laws and Regulations of 1825* indicated that the letters collected by a non-contract boat be turned in to the post office of the first town visited, but the terminus of the boat's run was where most mail was deposited, especially if the destination of the letter was the terminus town or beyond. The same PL&R set a fee of 2¢ to be paid the captain of the ship for his services (at Lake Erie ports the fee was 1¢). Some post offices charged the addressee this fee on prepaid letters, others did not. From the middle of 1851 until the end of 1852 this 2¢ charge to the addressee was made mandatory.

---

*See the articles by Henry A. Meyer for a full report on the classes of waterways mail in the following issues of the *S. P. A. Journal:* Sept., 1949; Oct., 1949; Feb., 1950; June, 1950; March, 1951. See also his article, "The Collecting of Steamboat Covers," *Stamps* (August 1, 1953).

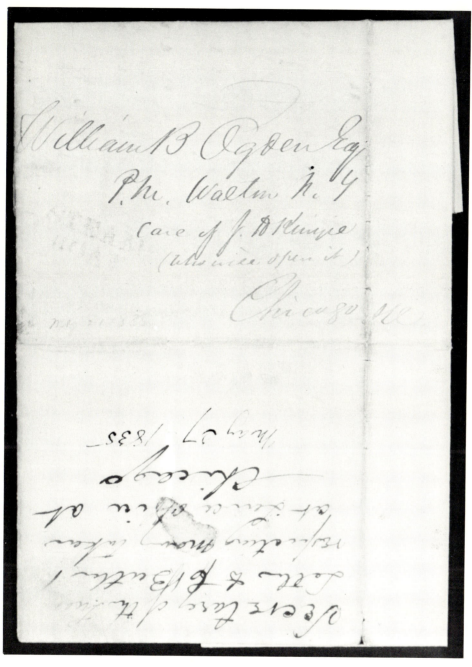

Letter addressed to William B. Ogden, Chicago, from Sec'y of Treasury Levi Woodbury dated May 27, 1835, with red STEAM/BOAT.

Blue circle Buffalo, N.Y., postmark dated OCT 20 (1843), with ms. rate marking, and blue STEAMBOAT in fancy scroll. Letter from William B. Ogden, Chicago's first mayor, and dated October 14, was placed aboard lake steamer prior to departure and then put in mails upon arrival at Buffalo.

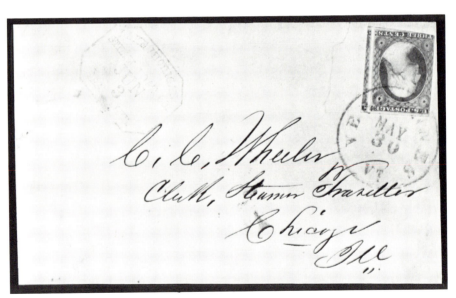

Steamboat cover to Chicago from Vermont origin, with dated marking of LAKE MICH-IGAN STEAM BOAT CO. Ship TRAVELLER JUN 3, used with 3 cents 1851 stamp.

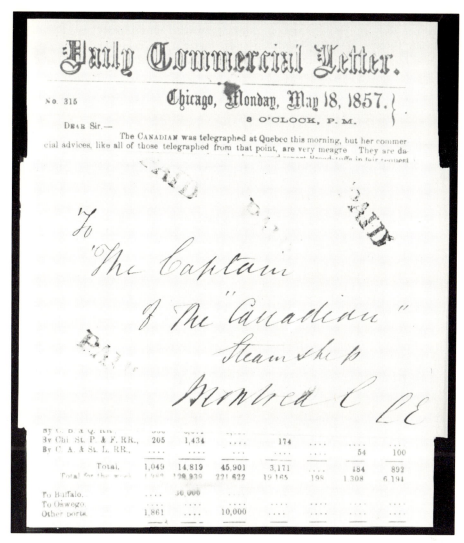

DAILY COMMERCIAL LETTER dated May 18, 1857, sent PAID to Captain of Steamship "Canadian" at Montreal.

Unpaid steamboat letters were treated as "Ship" letters, a different category of mail, with a fee of 2¢ plus the 3¢ inland postage if addressed beyond the town where deposited in the post office, or 6¢ if addressed to that town. These fees were made uniform in 1861 when the ship fee to port of arrival was made 5¢.

In 1863 the rate for unpaid steamboat letters was fixed at double the domestic rate. On prepaid letters some postmasters again imposed a 2¢ steamboat fee, while others charged another full rate of postage, or 3¢.

Postal markings from Chicago and other Great Lakes ports that indicate waterway use are not plentiful. Manuscript markings were used on the early stampless letters. When handstamps were employed, varieties in size, type, color, and design or figure were used by the different cities rather than a uniform marking. The Great Lakes cities

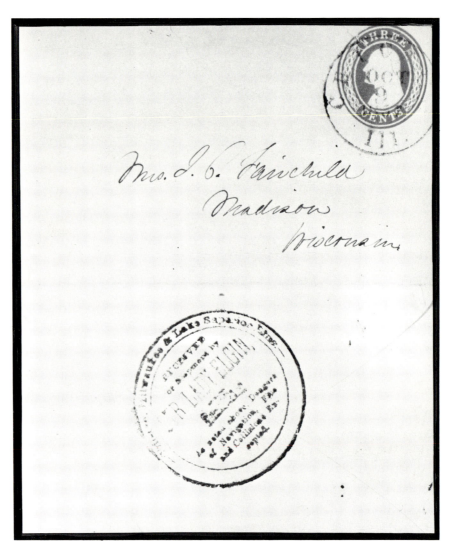

Receiving mark of GREAT LAKES STEAMBOAT "STR. LADY ELGIN" on 3 cents entire Nesbitt issue cancelled by year dated postmark OCT 9 1857. Steamer sank September 8, 1860, en route from Chicago to Milwaukee following collision with lumber schooner.

used the markings "Steamboat," "Steam" or "Ship" although the Chicago post office is not known to have used "Ship." Theron Wierenga, writing in *Stamps* (Jan. 24, 1970) notes that Chicago used a marking that read "STEAM" composed of Gothic letters measuring 18×4, in the 1850's. Konwiser reported an 1850 straight-line "STEAM" (and 10) in blue and green earlier. (*Stamps,* Jan. 18, 1941)

The "STEAMBOAT" markings used by Chicago are usually straightline in Gothic (sans serif) letters of varying sizes. Their use ranged from the 1850's until the early 1870's, and are found in both black and in blue. Three sizes have been noted, although there may be others: 37×5, 43×5, and 40×6. Henry A. Meyer (*S.P.A. Journal,* Oct. 1949) records the use of a 26 mm. single line circle marking containing small Gothic "STEAMBOAT" in the upper portion, and used in 1872.

Inland and coastal waterway mail often carry markings containing the name of the boat. These "Packet Marks" were often applied by the purser of a ship carrying passengers, often a contract mail carrier, and were used to advertise the ship's name. Some markings incorporate the ship's name with "Steamboat," but generally they do not have postal significance.

Blue double circle postmark dated RA OCT 16 (1863) and cork cancels on two 3 cents 1861 stamps, and blue STEAMBOAT on envelope addressed to Michigan.

Black circle postmark dated OCT 18 (1867) and cork cancels on two 3 cents 1861 stamps, and black STEAMBOAT on envelope addressed to New York State.

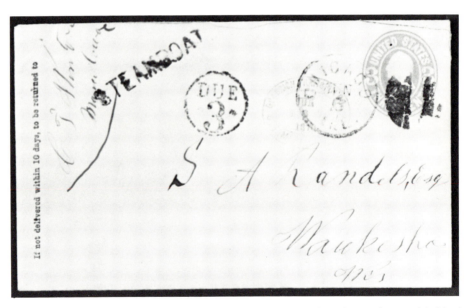

Black circle postmark dated JUN 6 (1870) on 3 cents entire of 1864 issue with black circle "DUE 3," and black STEAMBOAT; blue double oval marking "GOODRICH TRANSP'N CO./STEAMER MANITOWOC" on envelope addressed to Wisconsin.

Black circle postmark dated MAY 12 (1870 period) and black cork cancel on pair 3 cents 1869 stamps, with black STEAMBOAT. Late use of this marking on letter addressed to Chicago, origin unknown.

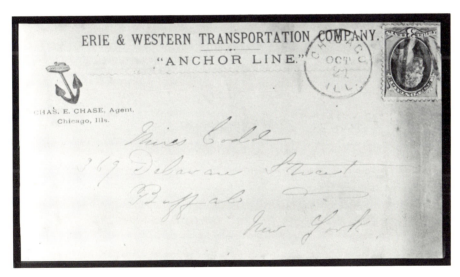

Chicago Steamboat c.c. of ANCHOR LINE—ERIE & WESTERN TRANSPORTA- TION CO., on cover with 3 cents Banknote issue postmark dated OCT 21 (1872 period).

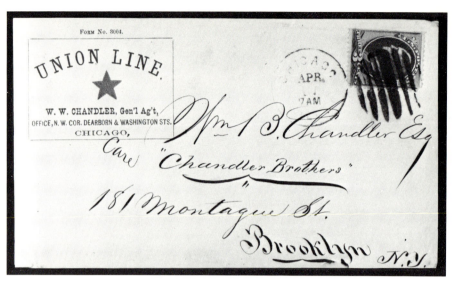

Chicago Steamboat c.c. of UNION LINE—W. W. CHANDLER, Gen'l Ag't. on cover
with 3 cents Banknote stamp and postmark dated APR 17 (1872 period).

CHICAGO AND THE HANDLING OF FOREIGN MAIL

Most American communities in the 19th century were affected by the stream of immigrants from both overseas lands and from other parts of America that settled in or passed through their territory. As the interior of the United States was settled and developed, the personal and commercial communications with Europe and the rest of the world were regularized. During the first half of the century postal arrangements for Chicago and most inland places provided for letters to be delivered to New York, Boston, or other Atlantic ports where the post offices provided exchange facilities between the United States and other countries. The postal conventions of treaties between the United States and Great Britain of 1848–1849, with Bremen and Hamburg in 1851, and with France in 1857, standardized these postal procedures.

Folded letter to France with paid markings and red circle postmark dated 24 OCT (1850) at 21 cents rate. (Enlarged)

139

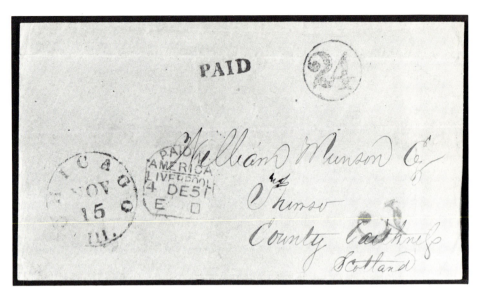

Cover to Scotland with circle postmark dated NOV 15 (1851), PAID, U.S. inland post-age mark "3" and circled rate "24," and LIVERPOOL transit mark, all markings in red.

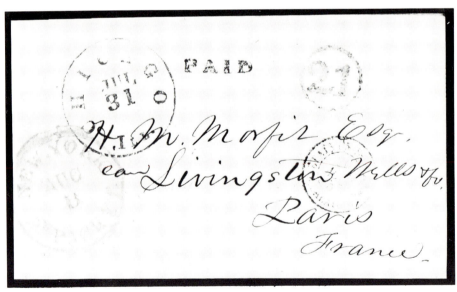

Cover to France with black circle postmark dated JUL 31 (1855) and black PAID; red "NEW YORK AM. PACKET" and circled rate mark "21."

140

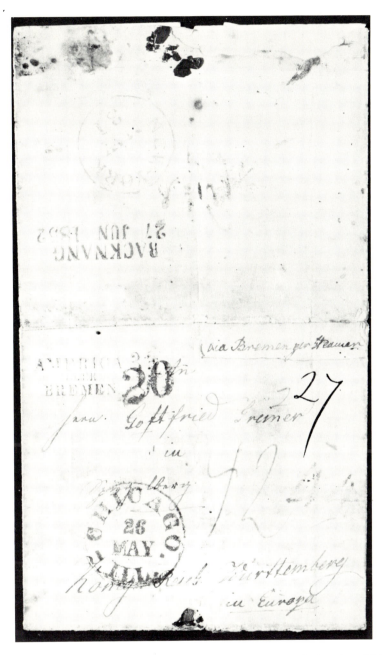

Unpaid folded letter to German States with red circle postmark dated 26 MAY (1852) via Bremen Treaty at 27 cents rate. Letter carried by Havre Liner "Humboldt" illustrates transit, credit, and local rate markings. (Enlarged)

Cover to Belgium with dated postmark JUN 4 1856 tying 12 cents and strip of three 3 cents stamps of 1851 paying 21 cents rate; handstamped "U.S. PKT" in black and "NEW YORK AM. PKT." in red; with Belgian receiving mark and rates in manuscript.

In 1857, the United States exchange offices for the British and French mails were New York, Boston, Philadelphia, and San Francisco; the British offices were London, Liverpool, and Southampton; the French offices were Havre and the travelling office from Calais to Paris. For Prussian closed mail, carried in closed pouches via England by British and American packet boats, the exchange offices were New York and Boston, and the French office of exchange was Aix-la-Chapelle (Aachen).

Chicago was added to the list of exchange offices for the various categories of foreign mail shortly thereafter. Tracy Simpson (in his *United States Postal Markings 1851 to 1861*) notes that Chicago participated in British mail arrangements from December 14, 1859. A notice in the *Chicago Press and Tribune* of July 25, 1860, carried the following announcement:

> *New Postal Arrangement.* The Chicago Post Office has just been constituted an office of Exchange on the part of the United States for the exchange of mails with Glasgow Scotland in sealed bags. The Post Office is now in direct communication with London, Liverpool, Dublin, Londonderry and Glasgow. The mails made up for those cities are dispatched every Thursday morning by the Grand Trunk (Canadian) steamers.

For their overseas delivery, mails made up at Chicago were dispatched by American packets (steamships of United States or even Canadian, British, or German registry under contract with the United States to carry its mails) running between Portland and Great Britain in winter, and between Quebec or Riviere du Loup and Britain in summer. Mail so carried was rated as "Am. Pkt." On May 9, 1861, Chicago was added as an exchange office for the Prussian closed-mail arrangement, where mail was carried via British and American packets, through England and Belgium to Aachen and beyond. Similarly, Chicago became an exchange office for the French postal arrangement on March 18, 1861, and mail was rated as by British packet. Chicago was not an exchange office under the Hamburg or the Belgian closed-mail arrangements.

In general outgoing mail or letters received from abroad with postage wholly unpaid, or prepaid only to the American port of entry, were marked in black with a Chicago exchange office postmark and the amount of unpaid postage to be collected at the U.S. post office of destination. Fully prepaid mail was marked in red. In addition, incoming or outgoing mail carried numerals or other markings denoting a credit to the foreign country by the U.S. were in red and debit markings in black. The Chicago exchange office also employed a blue routing mark showing "CHICAGO," the date, routing (i.e., by Am. Pkt. or Br. Pkt.) This circular mark, with or without a numeral, indicated that Chicago handled the incoming mail and that a sum, usually for inland postage, was to be collected from the addressee. The variety of foreign mail cancellations on incoming or outgoing mail associated with any American city is an attractive collecting specialty itself.

Mail between the United States and Canada, and other British North American areas, was handled on a different basis than ordinary foreign mail. Beginning in 1851, special "U. STATES" markings were applied on letters going into Canada, and exchange offices were established, mainly in border cities. Additions to the list of such offices and changes of exchange points took place from time to time so that through bags of mail could be sent without being opened at the border. It is not known exactly

Cover to Ireland, with black circle year dated postmark AUG 13 1858 on pair 12 cents 1851 stamps; with red New York "19" credit marking.

Prepaid folded letter to Egypt, with red circle year dated postmark NOV 9 1858, with PAID and various ms. rate markings. Handled by Prussian Closed Mail via U.K.

when Chicago was added to the list of Canadian exchange offices, but it was probably around 1859. Since substantially identical markings were sent to several exchange offices, the identification of an exchange office with specific exchange markings is known only in some cases. Between 1859 and 1868, mail from the Pacific Coast of the United States destined for Canada passing through the Chicago exchange office was marked with the distinctive circular route marking stamp containing "CHICAGO," the date, and the rate, "15."

During the period 1863 to 1878, the Post Office Department took measures to avert a loss of revenue due to inflation by securing legislation to permit the collection of unpaid postage on letters originating in foreign sources by specie or in adjusted depreciated paper currency. Thus, when a letter posted in Europe arrived at the Chicago exchange office, the relationship of gold to greenbacks on the day of receipt was multiplied by the amount of postage due. In addition, from 1868, postal conventions between the United States and other countries established a fine on unpaid letters to be assessed and retained by the country collecting the postage. Since this fine was assessed in U.S. notes, the unpaid letter fine was added to the adjusted postage due to indicate the amount collectible in U.S. notes or paper money on the date recorded. The Chicago exchange office did not have a stamp with dual rate markings, so that the amount to be collected in notes or currency was applied separately from the route marking.

Measures adopted by the Universal Postal Union went into effect July 1, 1875, for the signatory nations and widely affected rates and postal markings in the period that followed. Foreign mail was to be sent prepaid by adhesive or envelope stamps, the entire postage prepaid to be retained by the post office of the country of origin. The standard rate of postage was fixed at 5 cents (2-1/2 pence; 25 centimes) per one-half ounce (15 grammes), with postage due rates computed in gold centimes. Chicago foreign mail markings since 1875 are distinctive though not so varied as in the previous years.

144

Cover to England with black double circle postmark dated JUL 1 (1860) on pair 12 cents Type I 1857 stamps, and red credit marking "19."

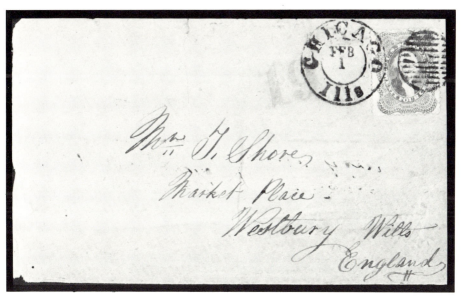

Cover to England with blue double circle postmark dated FEB 1 (1861) and attached grid on 24 cents 1860 stamp, with red Boston credit marking "19."

145

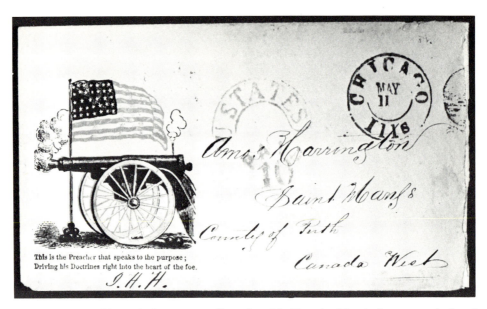

Stampless prepaid patriotic cover to Canada with blue double circle postmark dated MAY 11 (1861), and red arc "U. STATES" and "PAID 10."

Cover to Canada with black circle postmark dated OCT 19 (1865) and black star as cancel on 10 cents 1861 stamp; red oval exchange marking "U.S. 10 cts./PAID."

Cover illustrating Belgium Closed Mail Markings of 1865–1866 uses with New York Exchange Office handstamps; reverse side illustrates transportation via AM. PACKET and Belgian transit and receiving marks.

Cover to Switzerland with black circle postmark dated JAN 31 (1870) cork cancel on 10 cents and 3 cents 1869 stamps, and directional marking "VIA OSTENDE." Handstamp "INSUFFICIENTLY PAID" applied to indicate the shortage on 15 cents rate for any route except via France.

Prepaid cover to France during period without U.S.-Franco treaty arrangements, with black circle postmark dated SEP 19 (1870), via England showing 10 cents rate.

Cover to Germany with black circle postmark dated JUN 13 (1871), and with negative X cancel on 7 cents Banknote stamp. Letter directed to go by Hamburg steamer but went instead via Bremen due to shipping changes resulting from Franco-Prussian War.

Cover to Germany with black circle postmark dated SEP 15 (1870) and black cork cancel on 15 cents 1866 stamp, via New York and Bremen Treaty mail.

Cover to Switzerland with blue circle postmark dated OCT 9 (1873) with fancy (blue shield) cancel on 10 cents Banknote stamp; red New York Transit mark "VIA ENG. & OSTE."

Unpaid cover to France during period without U.S.-Franco treaty arrangements, with blue circle postmark dated OCT 11 (1873); has British rate marking "2F" and French ms. "12" decimes. Mail was sent to England and transmitted to France according to provisions of Franco-British treaty.

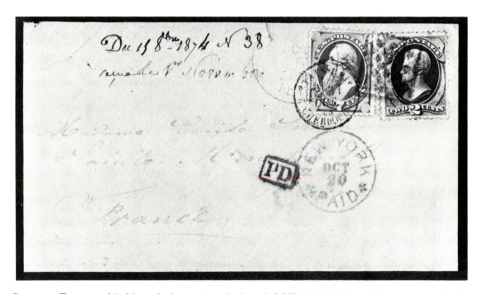

Cover to France with blue circle postmark dated OCT 15 (1874) and fancy cancel tying 7 cents and 2 cents Banknote stamps paying 9 cents rate, with N.Y.F.M. and CHER-BOURG exchange office markings.

150

Cover to Cuba with blue circle postmark dated JUN 8 (1876) and blue cancel circled "1" on 10 cents Banknote stamp, the postage rate for direct steamer mail (Enlarged).

Cover to Eastern India with blue circle postmark dated APR 1 (1876) with blue fancy (cross) cancel on pair 10 cents Banknote stamps, a 5 cents 1875 stamp, and 3 cents entire. The 28 cents rate paid postage via England, then overland through Brindisi and the Suez Canal. Cover shows various transit and forwarding marks.

151

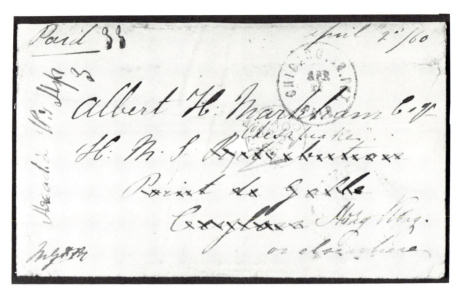

Cover Wisconsin to Asia via Chicago—Red circle Exchange Office marking CHICAGO AM. PKT. PAID APR. 11 (1860), paying 33 cents rate. Addressed to "H.M.S. Retribution" in Ceylon, and readdressed to "H.M.S. Chesapeake" at Hong Kong "or elsewhere," letter carried to Southampton and transhipped by British mail.

Cover Illinois to Germany via Chicago—Red circle Exchange Office marking CHICAGO ILL AM. PKT 7 PAID dated AUG 29 (1861), paying 30 cents Prussian Closed Mail rate on envelope with patriotic design.

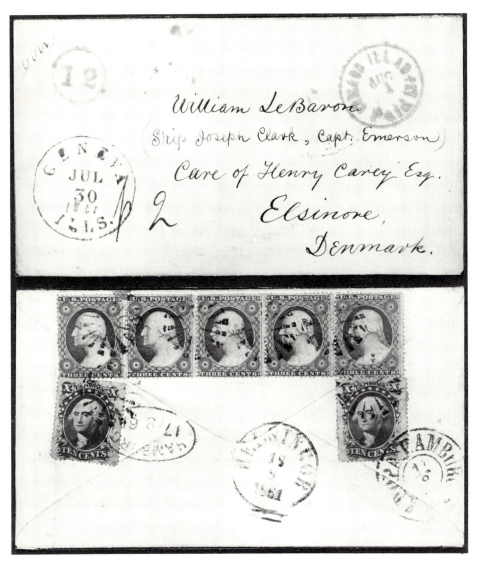

Cover Illinois to Denmark via Chicago—Red circle Exchange Office marking CHI-CAGO ILL. AM. PKT PAID dated AUG 1 1861; red circled "12" for Prussian credit. Reverse has Hamburg Packet and transit marks with 35 cents stamps of 1857 issue. Letter travelled Prussian Closed Mail to Hamburg rather than through Canada and Aachen, the usual route.

*Cover California to Canada via Chicago—Red circle Exchange Office marking CHI-
CAGO ILL PAID 15; with San Francisco cog cancel dated SEP 14 1862 on 10 cents
1861 stamp and 5 cents 1862 stamp.*

*Cover Illinois to France via Chicago—Black circle Exchange Office marking CHICAGO
ILL 3; letter is 15 cents unpaid, with 8 decimes postage due. Origin town postmark
dated DEC 19 (1865).*

Cover Michigan to Australia via Chicago—Red circle Exchange Office marking CHI-CAGO PAID 12, with origin town postmark dated MAR 30 1870; red London transit marking, and black Ballarat UNCLAIMED.

Cover Switzerland to Illinois via Chicago—Red circle Exchange Office marking CHI-CAGO ILL 21 dated SEP 13 (1862), with French and British transit and rate markings.

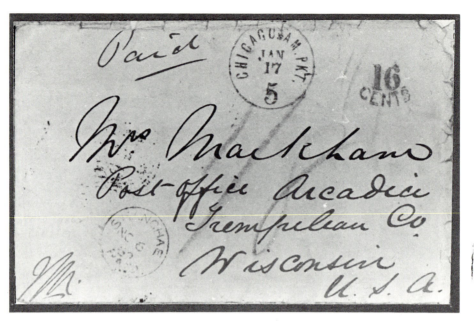

Cover China to Wisconsin via Chicago—Blue circle Exchange Office marking for handling fee CHICAGO AM. PKT 5 dated JAN 17 (1863); carried via Southampton, with 16 cents Transatlantic credit mark.

Cover England to Wisconsin via Chicago—Red circle Exchange Office marking CHICAGO AM. PKT 24 PAID dated JUL 19 (1863); with red "21 CENTS" credit mark.

Cover England to Wisconsin via Chicago—Blue circle Exchange Office marking CHI-
CAGO AM. PKT. 24 dated AUG 13 (1863); with blue circled "IN U.S. NOTES 28" and
black arc "3 CENTS."

Cover England to Illinois via Chicago—Blue circle Exchange Office marking CHICAGO
AM. PKT. 24 dated OCT 18 (1864); with red SL "INSUFFICIENTLY/PREPAID"
and blue "44 U.S. NOTES" and black arc "3 CENTS."

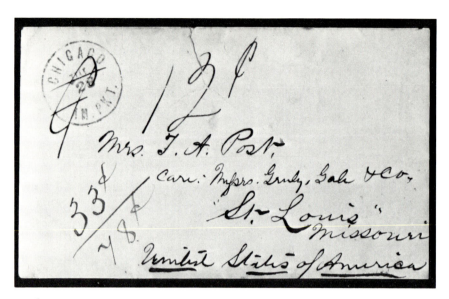

Cover Tangiers to St. Louis via Chicago—Blue circle Exchange Office marking CHI-CAGO AM. PKT. dated JUL 23 (1864). Letter from U.S.S. St. Louis via Gibraltar and England with 33 cents rate collect, and various debit and credit markings.

Cover South Australia to Wisconsin via Chicago—Blue circle Exchange Office and rate marking CHICAGO AM. PKT. 5 dated DEC 24 (1864), with blue unpaid marking "11 U.S. NOTES." Black Adelaide postmark dated SP 23 64 used as cancel, and with various red transit and credit markings.

158

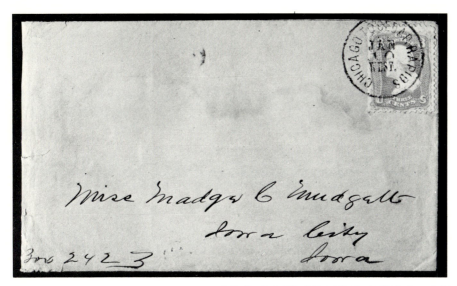

Railroad Marking—Blue circle marking CHICAGO TO CEDAR RAPIDS dated JAN 10 WEST (1860's) on 3 cent 1861 stamp, indicates shipment via Chicago and Northwestern R.R.

Railroad Marking—Black circle marking CHICAGO TO DAVENPORT dated JAN 1 (1866) on 3 cents 1861 stamp. (Enlarged).

163

Railroad Marking—Double circle marking CHICAGO TO ST. LOUIS dated SEP 8 1866 cancels 3 cents 1861 stamp.

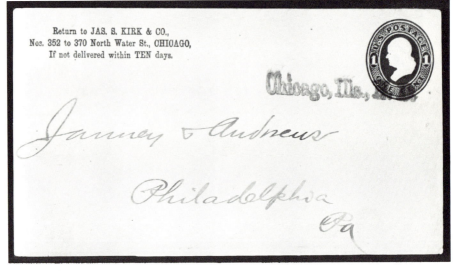

Railroad Marking—Black straight-line "Chicago, Ills. R.R." used as cancel on 1 cent Plimpton entire. Used on circular mail.

ple, nearly 60 million bushels of grain were handled. And like grain, the meat packing trade was on a prodigious scale. It was reported that in 1863 alone, the hogs processed in the city, if arranged in single file, would have reached New York. In 1869, the introduction of refrigerator cars and the development of the canning and preserving processes, widened the opportunities for Chicago packers.

The growing number of Chicago manufacturing plants also made an impressive contribution to the nation's economy. The iron industry developed in this period by bringing together Lake Superior ore, eastern or Illinois coal, and Michigan limestone, to form a variety of steel products. The nation's first steel rails were produced in 1865 by the North Chicago Rolling Mills. By 1870, McCormick reapers and other Chicago-made agricultural implements dominated American markets.

On October 8 and 9, 1871, a great fire swept across the heart of the city, destroying its entire commercial district and many of its neighborhoods in the west and north sides, and leaving a third of the people homeless. The building housing the post office, at Monroe and Dearborn Streets, like the other supposedly fireproof structures in the area, was gutted. Within a short time, temporary arrangements were made to handle the necessary welfare and relief activities and Chicago began to rebuild. Despite the destruction, the fire did not basically alter the shape or purposes of the city. Both rebuilding and confidence had grown to the point that by the Spring of 1872 Chicagoans began planning an exposition to call attention to their achievement. A huge glass and iron building was constructed on the present site of the Art Institute, between Adams and Jackson Streets on Michigan Avenue. When the exposition opened in September, 1873, more than 60,000 people were attracted during the 18 days of the exposition to view the exhibits featuring the "material and cultural progress of Chicago" as well as to see the rebuilt city itself.

Postmark and cancel used from April 10, 1868 to July 10, 1870, here ties two 2 cents Black Jack "Z" grill stamps. Probably represents overpayment on 3 cents rate.

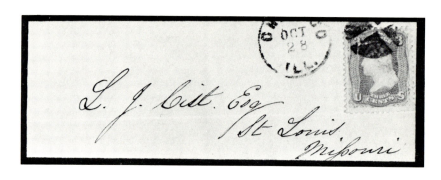

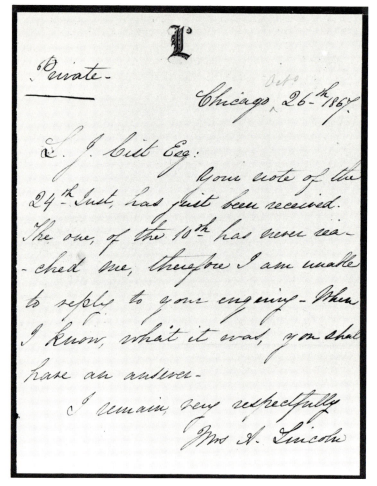

Chicago letter and cover (mourning stationery) used in October, 1867, written and signed by Mrs. Abraham Lincoln.

Registered Letter—Black circle "REGISTERED" dated APR 8 (1870). Indistinct black cancel ties 3 cents entire and 15 cents 1869 stamp. This Registration rate existed from January 1, 1869, to December 31, 1873, and was payable by affixed stamps.

Registered Letter—North District Station Registered postmark dated AUG 6, with blue "W" cancel on stamps of 1870–1871 issue.

The Chicago post office managed to survive its "ordeal by fire" in 1871 in creditable fashion. (See the account in the 1969 mimeographed booklet issued by Postmaster Henry W. McGee, "A Historical Account of the Chicago Post Office.") While the fire was burning out on Monday, October 9, mail was made up in the yard of C. S. Squires, the assistant postmaster, at the corner of Calumet Avenue and 26th Street. In a short time Postmaster Francis Eastman secured temporary quarters in Burlington Hall, at State and 16th Streets, and then moved three weeks later to the Methodist Church on Wabash and Harrison Streets, a location closer to the downtown district.

To avoid loss and confusion in the handling of mail all railroad cars from the Chicago division of the railway mail service were called in by telegraph and sidetracked on yards free of fire danger. The substations about the city were organized as main delivery units for the major divisions of the postal system and collection boxes were set up on street cars and in convenient locations. The city post office personnel claimed that the fire did not cause them to lose a single letter. A more permanent organization found the city divided into 122 carrier districts or routes, handled by a staff of approximately 130 carriers and 27 clerks.

Chicago's growth after the fire was reflected in Post Office Department reports. As early as January, 1872, the *Postal Record* asserted that the business transactions of the Chicago post office ranked second in the nation. This report emphasized the importance of the city as a center for the distribution of mails accumulating from every section of the country. On several occasions, it was stated, a hundred tons of mail matter were handled on a single day, and that about twenty large wagons were required to transport this volume between the post office and the various railroad depots.

The Chicago postmarks used from about 1865 to 1877 consisted of a single circle struck in black or blue, and ranging in diameter from 23 mm. to 27 mm. Different arrangements are found in the spacing of the letters and the center position of the date. From 1873 to 1877, circles with diameters of 26 mm. and 27 mm. were used as they usually included an hour designation. No year designation is found in these postmarks. The townmarks found on first class mail were used with a wide variety of cork or wood cancels, with blue the dominant color used after 1873. More than 250 blue cancellations have been recorded, in designs that include geometrics, pictorials, initials, numerals, pinwheels, grids, and numerous miscellaneous patterns that were apparently limited only by the artistic execution of the maker. Most of these hand-cut cancellers wore rapidly and frequent changes were necessary, often as many as several times a week. They make an attractive field of study for the postmark specialist. From about January, 1878, until 1892 (when machine cancellations came into use), the townmarks were combined on one handle with standardized numeral or branch designation killer cancels, and were struck from metal dies. From this point the usual color of Chicago postmarks was black.

Chicago Blue circle postmark dated MAY 11 and 3-leaf-clover cancel on 3 cents 1873 stamp.

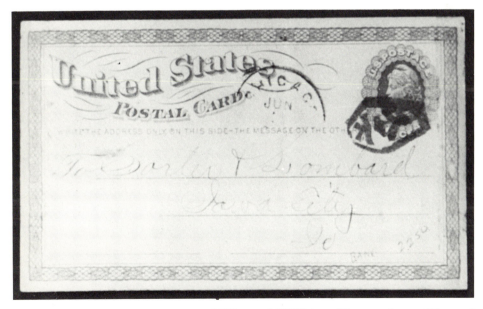

Chicago Blue circle postmark dated JUN 3 and KKK-in-coffin cancel on 1873 postal card.

Chicago Blue circle postmark dated 19 NOV and anchor-in-diamond-frame cancel on 1873 postal card.

Chicago Blue circle postmark dated 2 OCT and shield-in-octagon-frame cancel on 1873 postal card.

Chicago Blue circle postmark dated 16 OCT and gin-barrel cancel on 1873 postal card.

Chicago Blue circle postmark dated MAR 30 and pool-table cancel on 1873 postal card.

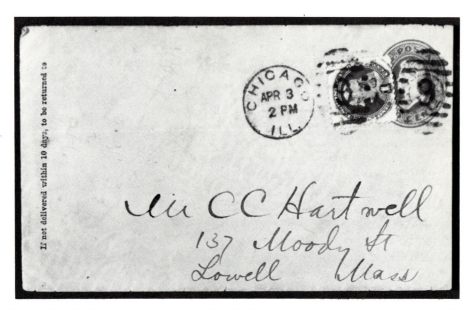

Cover with black circle postmark dated APR 3 (1880) and attached standardized killer cancel on 2 cents entire and 1 cent 1880 reissue of 1869 stamp. Some variation of this arrangement of townmark and cancel used from January 8, 1878, until 1892 when machine cancellations came into use.

172

CITY POSTMARKS AND
POST OFFICE EXPANSION*

Many collectors who specialize in the postmarks of one city have a fondness for townmarks of postoffices later incorporated into their favorite. There is no more fertile field for this phase of philately than that offered by the city of Chicago.

A very rough estimate would indicate that there were more than 200 individual post-office names in the towns and communities which have been absorbed by this city. Here also will be found the very unusual situation in which large numbers of independent postoffices existed for years within the city limits but without any connection with the Chicago postoffice. Such a condition where one or two such offices might exist may not have been uncommon but in Chicago at one period there were about 60 such post-offices.

Chicago had a record growth in population after the great fire of 1871 with practically no increase in area and came to be surrounded by thriving cities and villages. The great annexation of 1889 and the smaller additions of the next four years increased the area of the city from 36.15 to 182.92 square miles, an addition of more than 400 percent. (Ed. note: see accompanying map showing Chicago growth.)

This area was not quickly taken into the sphere of influence of the Chicago postoffice for in June, 1893, it was serving only about 63 square miles while the remaining 120 square miles of corporate area was being handled by the 60 independent postoffices.

In June, 1893, most of these offices had been within the city limits for four years, although there is a possibility that a few were established after the annexations. During the first half of 1889 the Chicago postoffice served a maximum area of 36.15 square miles. This is based on an assumption that the entire city which had grown but a single square mile since 1869 was being served by the postoffice.

In the four years from 1889 to 1893 the postoffice had expanded to include 27 additional square miles—4.5 miles in Lake View, 13.5 in Hyde Park and the Stockyards Dictrict, 7 square miles in South Chicago, and 1.5 square miles in Brighton Park. The three larger areas mentioned were being served by the new Lake View, Hyde Park, Stockyards, and South Chicago postal stations.

---

*Edited version of article by Richard McP. Cabeen that appeared in *Philately* (16 December 1946). The editor prepared the tables showing the "Expansion of Jurisdiction of Chicago Post Office" and "Independent Post Offices That Became Part of the Chicago Post Office System."

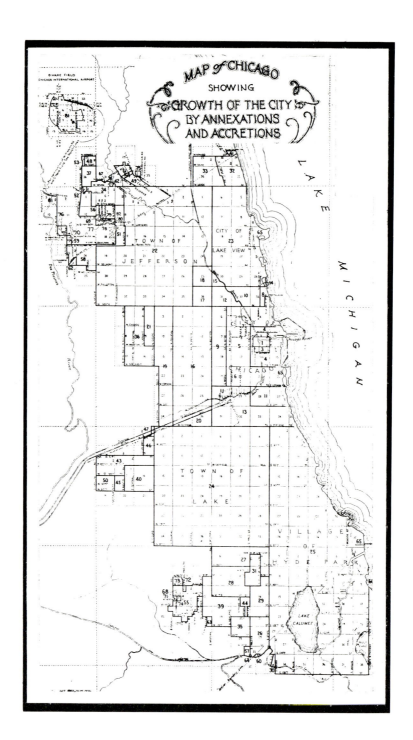

MAP of CHICAGO SHOWING GROWTH OF THE CITY BY ANNEXATIONS AND ACCRETIONS

174

GROWTH OF CHICAGO

Map No.	Area Included	Date of Act	Date in Effect	Area (sq. mi.)
1	Original Town platted by Canal Comrs	8-4-1830	8-4-1830	.42
	(Town of Chicago as organized—)	8-12-1831	8-12-1831	
2	Extension by Trustees	11-6-1833	11-6-1833	.67
3	Extension by Trustees	11-6-1833	11-6-1833	.88
4	TOWN of CHICAGO as incorporated	2-11-1835	2-11-1835	2.53
5	CITY OF CHICAGO as incorporated	3-4-1837	3-4-1837	10.19
6	Withdrawn by Legislature	1-21-1843	1-21-1843	9.69
7	Withdrawn by Legislature	3-3-1843	3-3-1843	9.31
6	Re-annexed by Legislature			
7	Re-annexed by Legislature			
8	Extension by Legislature	2-14-1851	2-14-1851	10.50
9	Extension by Legislature			13.50
10	Extension by Legislature			14.88
11	Extension by Legislature	2-12-1853	2-12-1853	17.49
12	Extension by Legislature			18.66
13	Extension by Legislature	2-13-1863	2-13-1863	23.71
14	Annexed as part of Lincoln Park by Legislature	2-8-1869	2-8-1869	23.79
15	Extension by Legislature			24.06
16	Extension by Legislature	2-27-1869	2-27-1869	35.15
17	Annexed by Ordinance: Vill. of	2-21-1887	4-22-1887	
	Jefferson & City of Chicago	5-16-1887	5-25-1887	36.15
18	Annexed by Resolution Cook County			37.15
19	Annexed by Resolution Cook County			42.40
20	Annexed by Resolution Cook County	4-29-1889	5-20-1889	43.31
21	Part of Town of Cicero by election	6-29-1889	7-15-1889	44.31
22	Town of Jefferson by election	6-29-1889	7-15-1889	74.17
23	City of Lake View by election	6-29-1889	7-15-1889	84.48
24	Town of Lake by election	6-29-1889	7-15-1889	120.48
25	Village of Hyde Park by election	6-29-1889	7-15-1889	168.67
26	Part of Vill. of Gano by election	4-1-1890	4-21-1890	170.46
27	South Englewood by ordinance	5-12-1890	5-12-1890	173.38
28	Washington Heights by election	11-4-1890	11-4-1890	176.19
29	West Roseland by election	11-4-1890	11-4-1890	178.00
30	Annexed by Ordinance	12-4-1890	12-4-1890	178.05
31	Fernwood by election	4-7-1891	4-7-1891	179.07
32	Rogers Park by election	4-4-1893	4-4-1893	180.75
33	West Ridge by election	4-4-1893	4-4-1893	182.92
34	Norwood Park by election	11-7-1893	11-7-1893	185.02
35	Part of Town of Calumet by Ordinance	2-25-1895	2-25-1895	186.02
36	Austin by election	4-4-1899	4-4-1899	189.52
37	Edison Park by election	11-8-1910	11-8-1910	190.20
38	Disconnected by Ordinance	7-17-1911	7-17-1911	190.18
39	Morgan Park by election	4-7-1914	4-21-1914	193.30
40	Clearing by election	4-6-1915	4-24-1915	195.18
41	Annexed by Ordinance: Part of City	11-17-1914		
	of Evanston & City of Chicago	2-8-1915	5-5-1915	195.30
42	Annexed at Election	4-6-1915	5-13-1915	195.32
43	Part of Stickney by election	6-7-1915	9-3-1915	197.58
44	Extension by Legislature	7-1-1915	7-1-1915	197.90
45	Part of Stickney by election	11-6-1917	2-4-1918	198.27
46	Part of Stickney by election	4-5-1921	7-8-1921	198.76
47	Part of Stickney by Ordinance	5-20-1921	7-8-1921	198.79
48	Part of Maine Twp by election	6-5-1922	8-9-1922	199.08
49	Part of Niles Twp by election	11-7-1922	1-3-1923	199.42
50	Part of Stickney by election	4-3-1923	6-30-1923	200.18
51	Part of Norwood Park by election	4-8-1924	6-3-1924	201.12
52	Part of Norwood Park by election	4-8-1924	6-3-1924	201.18
53	Part of Maine Twp by election	4-8-1924	6-3-1924	201.26
54	Part of Niles Twp by election	4-8-1924	6-3-1924	201.48
55	Mount Greenwood by election	2-22-1927	2-22-1927	203.45
56	Part of Norwood Park by election	6-6-1927	8-1-1927	204.97
57	Part of Calumet by election	6-6-1927	8-1-1927	205.09
58	Part of Leyden Twp by Ordinance	2-29-1928	4-2-1928	206.59
59	Part of Norwood Park by Ordinance	2-29-1928	4-2-1928	206.65
60	Part of Calumet by Ordinance	5-9-1928	6-28-1928	206.67
61	Part of Niles Twp by Ordinance	5-28-1928	7-7-1928	206.97
62	Part of River Grove by Ordinance	11-21-1929	2-5-1930	207.08
63	Beverly by election	11-4-1930	11-4-1930	207.20
64	Disconnected by Ordinance	11-24-1930	1-20-1931	207.20
65	Accretions to 1933	—	—	212.88
66	Erosions to 1933	—		212.82
67	Disconnected by Ordinance	6-14-1935	7-12-1935	212.81
68	Annexed by Ordinance	3-3-1940	6-4-1940	212.86
69	Annexed by Ordinance	5-3-1950	6-5-1950	212.92
70	Added by Forest Preserve Dist.	4-20-1954	4-20-1954	212.98
71–	Annexed by Ordinances	4-7-1954		213.81
80			12-13-1955	
81	Annexed by Ordinance	3-28-1956	4-11-1956	221.37

Blue oval handstamp NORTH BRANCH P.O. used with blue double circle postmark dated APR 11 '64 and cut cork cancel on 3 cents 1861 stamp.

Blue oval handstamp WEST BRANCH P.O. used with blue double circle postmark dated JUN 6 '64 and cut cork cancel on 3 cents 1861 stamp.

Examples of Station Markings, 1870's.

177

Chicago postal stations of 1893 with carrier service are listed below and the number of carriers and size of areas served is noted.

	No. Carriers	Sq. Mi.
South Division	51	3.0
Cottage Grove	34	2.0
Hyde Park	15	6.0
Stockyards	40	5.9
South Chicago	17	7.0
World's Fair Sta.	26	1.25
Southwest	70	11.27
West Madison	63	6.94
Northwest	48	3.36
Lake View	26	4.25
West Division	33	1.0
Humboldt Park	16	2.5
North Division	73	3.65

The totals for the 13 stations show 512 carriers serving an area of a little more than 58 square miles. The downtown area served by the main postoffice is not included in these figures.

The following tables are also of interest because they provide the name and location of the main post office and the individual branch offices as they were started and as they changed addresses. Beginning with the establishment of the first branch in 1862, selected years to 1905 were used. This information was compiled from annual reports of the post office, directories, and newspaper accounts, and presents an interesting panorama of Chicago growth during those years.

The second table includes a list of more than 100 independent post offices that became part of the Chicago post office system, together with the dates of their establishment, their closing, and their approximate location. There may have been others but records of their existence are indefinite. "The cancellations of any of the 60 offices dated after the annexation," notes Cabeen, are "something better than postmarks of cities which became part of Chicago. They are the postmarks of offices maintaining an existence within the city itself."

EXPANSION OF JURISDICTION OF CHICAGO POST OFFICE

1862	1863	1871

Main
  Monroe & Dearborn
	Main	Main—South Division
		  temp. Wabash & Harrison

West Branch
  201 W. Randolph
	West Branch	West Division
		  Washington & Halsted

	North Branch Clark & Ontario	North Division

EXPANSION OF JURISDICTION OF CHICAGO POST OFFICE
Continued

1874	1878	1888
Main	Main	Main
Dearborn & Adams		Clark & Jackson
West Division	West Division	West Division
North Division	North Division	North Division
	355 N. Clark	
North West Division	North West Station	North West Station
517 Milwaukee		
South Division	South Division	South Division
3217 S. State		
South West Station	South West Station	South West Station
543 Blue Island		
	Stock Yards Station	Stock Yards Station
	42nd & Halsted	
		West Madison St. Sta'n.
		981 W. Madison
		Cottage Grove Station
		3729 Cottage Grove

1890	1893	1894
Main	Main	Main
	temp. quarters	temp. quarters
West Division	West Div. Sta.	West Div. Sta.
North Division	North Div. Sta.	North Div. Sta.
		357 N. Clark
North West Sta'n	North West Sta.	North West Sta.
South Division	South Div. Sta.	South Div. Sta.
South West Sta'n.	South West Sta.	South West Sta.
		18th & Blue Island
Stock Yards Sta'n	Stock Yards Sta.	Stock Yards Sta.
W. Madison St. Sta.	W. Madison St. Sta.	W. Madison St. Sta.
Cottage Grove Sta'n	Cottage Grove Sta.	Cottage Grove Sta.
Lake View Sta'n	Lake View Sta.	Lake View Sta.
1353 Diversey		
Hyde Park Sta'n	Hyde Park Sta.	Hyde Park Sta.
142 E. 53rd		
Humboldt Park Sta.	Humboldt Park Sta.	Humboldt Park Sta.
1576 Milwaukee		
	South Chicago Sta.	South Chicago Sta.
	91st & Houston	
	World's Fair Sta.	Woodlawn Park Sta.
	Govt Bldg, Jackson Pk.	366 63rd St.
		22nd Street Sta.
		86 22nd St.

EXPANSION OF JURISDICTION OF CHICAGO POST OFFICE
Continued

1890	1893	1894
		Ogden Ave. Sta. 324 Ogden

1895	1900*	1905

Central
    temp. quarters
	Central
	    Washington & Michigan
		Central
		    Federal Building

Sta. C
    416 W. Madison
	Sta. C	Sta. C
		    1247 W. Madison

Sta. A.
    575 N. Clark
	Lincoln Park Sta.*
	    649 N. Clark
		Lincoln Park Sta.
		    1546 N. Clark

Sta. F.
    291 N. Carpenter
	Sta. F.	Carpenter St. Sta.
		    743 N. Carpenter

Sta. J
    3217 S. State
	Armour Sta.	Armour Sta.
		    3017 Indiana

Sta. H
    543 Blue Island
	Pilsen Sta.
	    671 Loomis
		Pilsen Sta.
		    1507 W. 18th St.

Sta. K 4193 S. Halsted	Stock Yards Sta.*	Stock Yards Sta.

Sta. D
    981 W. Madison
	Sta. D
	    833 W. Madison
		Sta. D
		    2108 W. Madison

Sta. M
    3729 Cottage Grove
	Sta. M
	    40th & Cott. Grove
		Sta. M
		    4235 Cottage Grove

Sta. B.
    1353 Diversey
	Lake View Sta.
	    1662 N. Clark
		Lake View Sta.
		    921 Belmont

Sta. N
    324 E. 55th St.
	Hyde Park Sta.	Hyde Park Sta.
		    1450 E. 55th St.

Sta. G
    1551 Milwaukee
	discontinued
	    9-3-00	

Sta. S
    234 91st St.
discontinued
	South Chicago Sta.*
	    9210 Commercial
		South Chicago Sta.

Sta. L
    2224 Cottage Grove
	22nd Street Sta.
	    90 E. 22nd St.
		20th Street Sta.
		    1929 Indiana

Sta. V
    1058 Millard
	Sta. V (Lawndale)	Hawthorne Sta.
		    3647 Ogden

Sta. E
    2021 W. Madison
	Garfield Park Sta.
	    1926 W. Madison
		Garfield Park Sta.
		    3907 W. Madison

Sta. O
    549 W. 63rd St.
	Englewood Sta.*	Englewood Sta.
		    449 W. 63rd St.

Sta. P
    606 W. 79th St.
	Auburn Park Sta.*	Auburn Park Sta.
		    612 W. 79th St.

1895	1900*	1905
Sta. R	Grand Crossing Sta.*	Grand Crossing Sta.
1143 75th St.		7427 So. Chicago
Sta. T	Pullman Sta.	Pullman Sta.
2370 115th St.	4 Arcade Bldg.	
Sta. U	Sta. U	Sta. U
Jackson & Canal		
Sta. W	Brighton Park Sta.*	McKinley Park Sta.
35th & Archer		3478 Archer
Sta. X	Ravenswood Sta.	Ravenswood Sta.
1250 E. Ravenswood		1812 Wilson
Sta. Y	Rogers Park Sta.	Rogers Park Sta.
4775 N. Clark	4796 N. Clark	1773 Lunt
West Pullman Sta.	West Pullman Sta.	West Pullman Sta.
750 W. 120th	12005 Halsted	
	Winnemac Sta.	North Halsted St. Sta.
	2536 Lincoln	2454 N. Halsted
	Edgewater Sta.	Edgewater Sta.
	1203 Bryn Mawr	5501 Broadway
	Douglas Park Sta.	Douglas Park Sta.
	580 S. Western	1207 S. Western
	Riverdale Sta.	Riverdale Sta.
	13565 Indiana	
	Washington Heights Sta.	Washington Heights Sta.
	1360 W. 103rd	1260 W. 103rd
	Elsdon Sta.	Elsdon Sta.
	3533 W. 51st St.	3435 W. 51st St.
	Chicago Lawn Sta.	Chicago Lawn Sta.
	3520 W. 63rd St.	3508 W. 63rd St.
	Irving Park Sta. (35)	Irving Park Sta.
	1159 Irving Park	4218 Irving Park
	Jefferson Sta.	Jefferson Sta.
	4303 Milwaukee	4841 Milwaukee
	Norwood Park Sta.	Norwood Park Sta.
	3470 Avondale	6040 Avondale
	Dunning Sta.	Dunning Sta.
	2684 W. Irving Park	6443 W. Irving Park
	Mont Clare Sta.	Mont Clare Sta.
	3315 W. Fullerton	Sayre & Medill
	Cragin Sta.	Cragin Sta.
	2984 Grand	4207 Armitage
	Clarkdale Sta.	
	8254 S. Central Park	

1895	1900*	1905
	Forest Hill Sta.	
	1751 W. 89th St.	
	Austin Sta.*	Austin Sta.
	5614 South Blvd.	433 N. Waller
	Hegewisch Sta.*	Hegewisch Sta.
	13305 Erie	
	East Side Sta.*	East Side Sta.
	9904 Ewing	9909 Ewing
	Dauphin Park Sta.*	Dauphin Park Sta.
	9033 Cottage Grove	8948 Cottage Grove
	Logan Square Sta.*	Logan Square Sta.
	1911 Milwaukee	2313 Milwaukee
	Wicker Park Sta.*	Wicker Park Sta.
	1263 Milwaukee	1633 Milwaukee
	Masonic Temple (31)#	Masonic Temple #
	51 State	159 N. State
	Stock Exchange (67)#	Stock Exchange #
	Washington & LaSalle	30 N. LaSalle
	South Water (80)#	South Water #
	15 LaSalle	207 N. LaSalle
	Monadnock (57)#	discontinued
	Dearborn & Jackson	
	Crilly (58)#	discontinued
	167 Dearborn	
	Board of Trade (56)#	Sheridan Park #
	117 Quincy St.	4476 Broadway
		Canal Sta.
		Northwestern Station
		Chicago Ave. Sta.
		210 W. Chicago
		51st Street Sta.
		5052 S. Halsted
		Jackson Park Sta.
		1113 E. 63rd
		Kinzie Sta.
		325 W. Kinzie
		Morgan Park Sta. Br.
		Morgan & Longwood
		Ogden Park Sta.
		1614 W. 63rd

*added during year 1900
stations without carriers

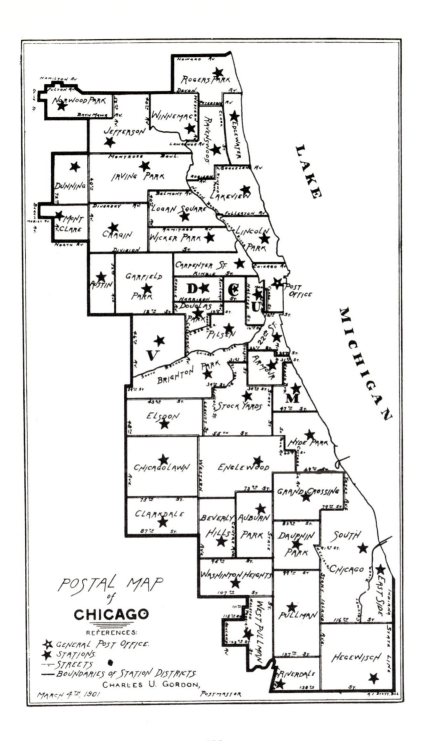

POSTAL MAP
of
CHICAGO
REFERENCES:
★ GENERAL POST OFFICE.
★ STATIONS.
--- STREETS
— BOUNDARIES OF STATION DISTRICTS.
CHARLES U. GORDON,
MARCH 4TH 1901   POSTMASTER

183

INDEPENDENT POST OFFICES THAT BECAME PART OF CHICAGO POST OFFICE SYSTEM

Post Office	Established	Discontinued	Approx. Location
AINSWORTH STATION			
See SOUTH CHICAGO			
ARGYLE PARK*	10-28-1885	6-6-1894	Winthrop Av & Argyle
AUBURN JUNCTION			
See AUBURN PARK			
AUBURN PARK*			
Est. as AUBURN JUNC-			
TION	3-19-1883		
To AUBURN PARK	4-10-1888	6-6-1894	79th & Wright
AUSTIN	4-5-1867	3-31-1900	Lake & Central
AVONDALE*	3-19-1880	6-6-1894	Kedzie & Belmont
BANDON	1-11-1884	3-25-1889	1594 Milwaukee Av
BOWMANVILLE*	6-2-1884	6-9-1894	Lincoln north @ 59th
BRAINERD STATION	2-13-1891	2-17-1893	87th & Ashland
BRIGHTON PARK			
Est. as FACTORYVILLE	10-8-1872		
To BRIGHTON PARK	6-27-1883	6-6-1894	Kedzie & 57th St.
BROOKLINE PARK*			
Est. as REDDY	6-20-1891		
To BROOKLINE PARK	10-7-1891	6-6-1894	7114 Cottage Grove
BROWNS MILL			
See CUMMINGS			
BUENA PARK*	11-1-1888	6-6-1894	Opp RR—near Graceland
BURNHAM	4-16-1890	8-30-1919	?
BURNSIDE CROSSING*	11-23-1888	6-6-1894	92nd & Cottage Grove
CALUMET (1)*	9-9-1835	6-6-1894	Clinton near 89th
CALUMET (2)			
See SOUTH CHICAGO			
CALUMET (3)			
See ROSELAND			
CENTRAL PARK*	6-19-1874	6-6-1894	4131 W Lake St
CHELTENHAM*	12-5-1884	6-6-1894	79th & Coles
CHICAGO LAWN*	12-24-1883	6-30-1894	63rd & Central Park
CICERO#	5-15-1867	2-15-1921	Independent Town
CLARKDALE JUNCTION*	6-11-1891	6-6-1894	83rd @ Central Park
CLEARING	7-1-1902	12-31-1916	67th & Cicero
COLEHOUR*	7-9-1875	6-6-1894	10301 Ave. K
CRAGIN*	9-12-1882	6-6-1894	Opp RR—Laramie & Gnd
CRAWFORD*	9-19-1884	6-6-1894	Butler near 24th
CUMMINGS*			
Est. as BROWNS MILL	5-9-1878		
To CUMMINGS	6-27-1882	6-6-1894	Torrance @ 107th

INDEPENDENT POST OFFICES THAT BECAME PART OF
CHICAGO POST OFFICE SYSTEM, Continued

Post Office	Established	Discontinued	Approx. Location
CUMMORN	5-10-1854	9-23-1859	
Became AUBURN JUNCTION			
DAUPHIN PARK*	5-21-1892	6-6-1894	89th Pl @ Cott. Gve
DREXEL	3-31-1894	6-30-1910	?
DUNNING*			
Est. as MONROE	5-11-1838		
To LEYDEN CENTER	7-6-1856		
To DUNNING	6-11-1883	6-6-1894	Cherry & Irving Pk
EDGEWATER*	1-3-1888	6-6-1894	RR Sta E Bryn Mawr
EDISON			
See EDISON PARK			
EDISON PARK	10-6-1890		
To EDISON	11-29-1895	3-31-1911	Higgins @ Narraganset
ELMWOOD PARK#	?	After 1931	Independent Village
ELSDON*	7-23-1889	6-6-1894	51st near Trumbull
ENGLEWOOD*			
Est. as JUNCTION GROVE	12-2-1861		
To ENGLEWOOD	11-29-1868	6-6-1894	6211 Wentworth
ENGLEWOOD HEIGHTS*	10-19-1889	6-6-1894	89th & Page
EVERGREEN PARK#	6-4-1875	After 1931	Independent Village
FACTORYVILLE			
See BRIGHTON PARK			
FERNWOOD*	2-14-1884	6-6-1894	103rd & Park
FOREST GLEN*	3-4-1884	6-6-1894	Elston & Forest Glen
FOREST HILL*	7-13-1885	6-6-1894	79th & Robey
GANO*	12-14-1887	6-6-1894	116th & Dearborn
GRAND CROSSING*	3-6-1872	6-6-1894	75th & Wilson
GROSS PARK	2-18-1886	3-15-1889	?
HAVELOCK*	12-13-1860	6-6-1894	Front & Cemetery
HEGEWISCH*	7-28-1884	6-6-1894	13303 So Chicago
HERMOSA*	11-6-1885	6-6-1894	Armitage @ Keeney
HIGH RIDGE*	12-11-1888	6-6-1894	Weber & C&NW RR
HOPE			
See ROSELAND			
HUMBOLDT PARK	2-25-1878	5-28-1889	North & Kedzie
HYDE PARK	3-23-1860	7-1-1889	53rd & Lake Park
IRVING PARK*	5-16-1872	6-6-1894	Crawford & Irving Park
JEFFERSON*	7-29-1846	6-6-1894	Milwaukee @ Maynard
JUDD*	10-29-1885	6-6-1894	93rd & Washington Av
JUNCTION GROVE			
See ENGLEWOOD			
KENSINGTON*	5-22-1872	6-6-1894	Kensington @ Front

Post Office	Established	Discontinued	Approx. Location
LAKE	6-25-1854	7-11-1856	?
LAKE VIEW	1-21-1869	5-2-1879	Ashland & Irving Pk
LEYDEN CENTER			
See DUNNING			
LINDEN PARK*	5-14-1890	6-6-1894	Robinson & Kinzie
LONGWOOD*	11-17-1890	6-6-1894	95th @ Wood
LOOMIS AVENUE*	9-24-1890	6-6-1894	89th & Loomis
MANDELL*	4-17-1888	6-6-1894	Laramie & Harrison
MAPLEWOOD*	6-11-1872	6-6-1894	Evergreen & Maplewood
MAYFAIR*	6-2-1882	6-6-1894	St. James @ Milwkee
MONROE			
See DUNNING			
MONT CLARE*	12-19-1873	6-30-1894	RR Sta—Oak Pk @ Gnd
MORELAND*	11-27-1882	6-6-1894	W 48th & Kinzie
MORGAN PARK	10-17-1878	12-31-1912	111th & Ashland
MOUNT GREENWOOD	2-3-1887	11-30-1927	111th & Kedzie
NORMAL PARK			
Est. as NORMALVILLE	11-13-1872		
To WOOSTER	3-4-1884		
To NORMAL PARK	3-20-1884	6-15-1887	Halsted & 67th
NORWOOD PARK	1-3-1870	6-20-1894	Bryn Mawr @ Harlem
PACIFIC*			
Est. as PACIFIC JUNT'N	9-25-1877		
To PACIFIC	5-14-1883	6-6-1894	RR Sta—North & Crawfd
PARK MANOR*	5-11-1888	6-6-1894	6760 So Chicago
PARKSIDE	4-23-1883	2-16-1892	?
PULLMAN*	2-24-1887	6-6-1894	112th & Morse
RAVENSWOOD*	4-27-1869	6-6-1894	E Rvswd Pk & Wilson
REDDY			
See BROOKLINE PARK			
RIVERDALE*	2-16-1874	6-6-1894	136th & Indiana
ROGERS PARK	7-2-1873	6-6-1894	Near 6600 N Ashland
ROSELAND*			
Est. as HOPE	12-21-1854		
To CALUMET	9-19-1864		
To ROSELAND	2-16-1874	6-6-1894	Michigan & Union
SIMONS*	3-4-1886	6-6-1894	Kimball & Bloomgdle
SOUTH CHICAGO*			
Est. as CALUMET	12-27-1853		
To AINSWORTH STATION	10-7-1857		
To SOUTH CHICAGO	5-31-1871	4-1-1893	9150 So Chicago
SOUTH ENGLEWOOD*	6-24-1874	6-6-1894	RI RR—76th & Wallace

INDEPENDENT POST OFFICES THAT BECAME PART OF
CHICAGO POST OFFICE SYSTEM, Continued

Post Office	Established	Discontinued	Approx. Location
SOUTH LYNNE*	6-13-1877	6-6-1894	65th & Ashland
STOCK YARDS	9-5-1866	6-13-1870	43rd & Halsted
SUMMERDALE*	10-26-1887	6-6-1894	N 59th & Ravwd Pk
TRACY*	4-9-1891	6-6-1894	103rd & Wood
WASHINGTON HEIGHTS*	10-25-1869	6-6-1894	Vincennes & 103rd
WEST PULLMAN	6-22-1892	6-20-1894	State near 115th
WILDWOOD	1-5-1885	4-2-1891	?
WINDSOR PARK*	8-20-1891	6-6-1894	75th & Ford
WOODLAWN PARK	4-8-1884	2-15-1892	63rd & Stony Is
WOOSTER See NORMAL PARK			
WRIGHTS GROVE	11-11-1875	3-15-1889	In Lake View
WYGANT	3-13-1894	7-11-1894	?

Notes: *within Chicago city limits in 1893 but operated independently of Chicago post office.
not in Chicago city limits but served by Chicago post office.

AUSTIN—black ms. marking dated "Sept. 19 1867" with pen cancel on 3 cents 1861 stamp.

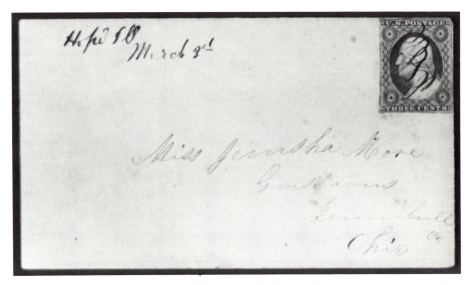

HOPE—black ms. marking dated "March 3" (1855 period), and pen cancel with P.M. initials on 3 cents 1851 stamp.

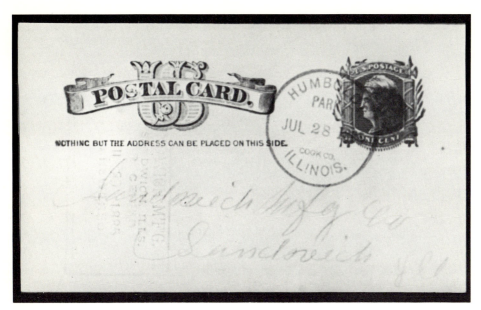

HUMBOLDT PARK— purple circle county year dated marking JUL 28 1885 on 1875 issue postal card.

JEFFERSON—black double circle dated DEC 1 (1876 period), with circled "US" as cancel on 3 cents Banknote stamp.

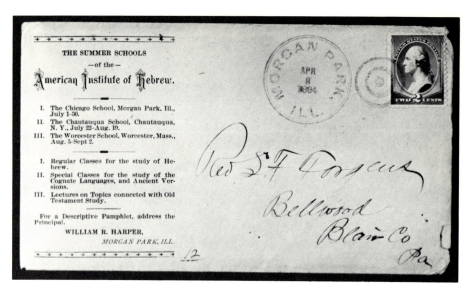

MORGAN PARK—blue-black double circle year dated postmark APR 8 1884, with target cancel on 2 cents Banknote stamp.

ROSELAND—black circle year dated postmark JAN 23 1883, with circled star cancel on 3 cents Banknote stamp.

STOCK YARDS—black double circle county postmark dated MAY 29 1867, with split cork design cancel on 3 cents 1861 stamp.

WOODLAWN PARK—black circle year dated postmark JAN 15 1886 with circle cancel on 2 cents Banknote stamp.

191